# EYEWITNESS
# FLIGHT

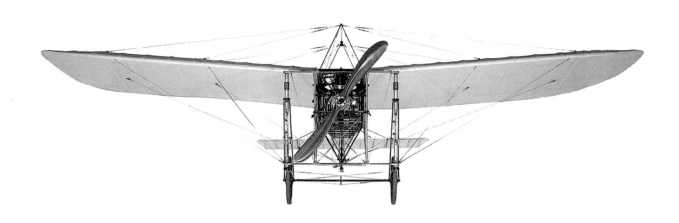

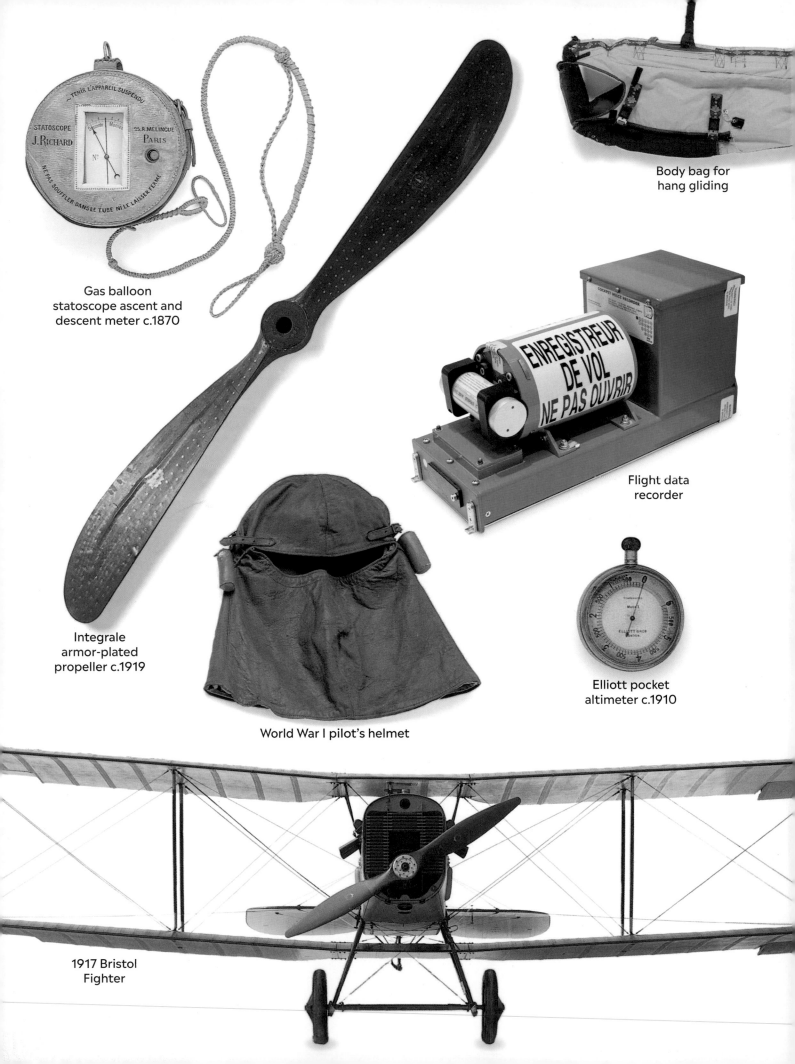

Gas balloon
statoscope ascent and
descent meter c.1870

Body bag for
hang gliding

Flight data
recorder

Integrale
armor-plated
propeller c.1919

World War I pilot's helmet

Elliott pocket
altimeter c.1910

1917 Bristol
Fighter

# EYEWITNESS
# FLIGHT

Written by
ANDREW NAHUM

Spring pressure
airspeed
indicator
c.1910

2006 Pegasus
flexwing ultralight

Stratolaunch
aircraft

1928 Hawker Hart
pressed-steel
landing wheel

1910 Anzani
aero-engine

**DK**

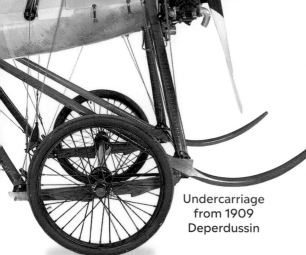

Undercarriage
from 1909
Deperdussin

Front fan from
Rolls-Royce Tay
turbofan engine

## REVISED EDITION

### DK DELHI
**Senior Editor** Rupa Rao
**Senior Art Editor** Vikas Chauhan
**Project Editor** Deeksha Micek
**Art Editor** Tanvi Sahu
**Assistant Picture Researcher** Nunhoih Guite
**Managing Editor** Kingshuk Ghoshal
**Managing Art Editor** Govind Mittal
**Senior DTP Designer** Harish Aggarwal
**DTP Designer** Vikram Singh
**DTP Coordinators** Jagtar Singh, Vishal Bhatia
**Production Editor** Pawan Kumar
**Jacket Designer** Rhea Menon
**Senior Jackets Coordinator** Priyanka Sharma Saddi

### DK LONDON
**Project Editor** Edward Pearce
**Senior Editor** Simon Mumford
**US Editor** Amber Williams
**US Executive Editor** Lori Cates Hand
**Managing Editor** Francesca Baines
**Managing Art Editor** Philip Letsu
**Production Controller** Jack Matts
**Senior Jackets Designer** Surabhi Wadhwa-Gandhi
**Jacket Design Development Manager** Sophia MTT
**Publisher** Andrew Macintyre
**Associate Publishing Director** Liz Wheeler
**Art Director** Karen Self
**Publishing Director** Jonathan Metcalf

**Consultant** Philip Whiteman

## FIRST EDITION

**Project Editor** John Farndon
**Art Editor** Mark Richards
**Senior Art Editor** Julia Harris
**Managing Editor** Sophie Mitchell
**Editorial Director** Sue Unstead
**Art Director** Anne-Marie Bulat
**Special Photography** Dave King, Peter Chadwick, Mike Dunning

This Eyewitness ® Guide has been conceived by
Dorling Kindersley Limited and Editions Gallimard

This American Edition, 2024
First American Edition, 1990
Published in the United States by DK Publishing
1745 Broadway, 20th Floor, New York, NY 10019

A catalog record for this book is available from the Library of Congress
ISBN 978-0-5938-4236-2 (Paperback)
ISBN 978-0-5938-4237-9 (ALB)

Printed and bound in China

**www.dk.com**

Mach meter c.1960

Engine parts from Henson and
Stringfellow's Aerial Steam
Carriage of 1845

1909 Paragon
experimental
propeller blade

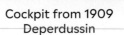

Cockpit from 1909
Deperdussin

# Contents

World War I
goggles

# Flying like a bird

People have always longed to take to the air, and history is filled with the stories of reckless souls who tried and failed to fly like birds. The 15th-century Italian artist and thinker Leonardo da Vinci recorded the most famous early thoughts about flying. Realizing that human arms were too weak to flap like birds, he filled his notebooks with ingenious ideas for flapping-wing machines called ornithopters.

### The first air crash?

In Greek legend, the inventor Daedalus made feather and wax wings for himself and his son, Icarus. When Icarus ignored his father's advice not to fly too high, the Sun melted the wax in his wings and he plunged into the sea.

### Flying ducks

In 1678, a French locksmith called Besnier tried to fly with wings that worked like the webbed feet of a duck. He was lucky to land alive.

*Netting support to be covered with bird feathers*

*Wooden wing frame*

**Abbas ibn Firnas**
Born in 810 in Al-Andalus (in modern-day Spain), Firnas may have built and flown a glider in the 9th century. However, the only record of his aeronautical activities, including ideas of covering himself in feathers to fly, appeared seven centuries after his death.

### How a bird flies

Most would-be aviators assumed that birds flew by flapping their wings down and backward, like rowing a boat. Leonardo devised mechanisms to replicate this, but in fact bird flight is much more complex. Scientists are still studying how and why birds change the shape and angle of their wings in flight.

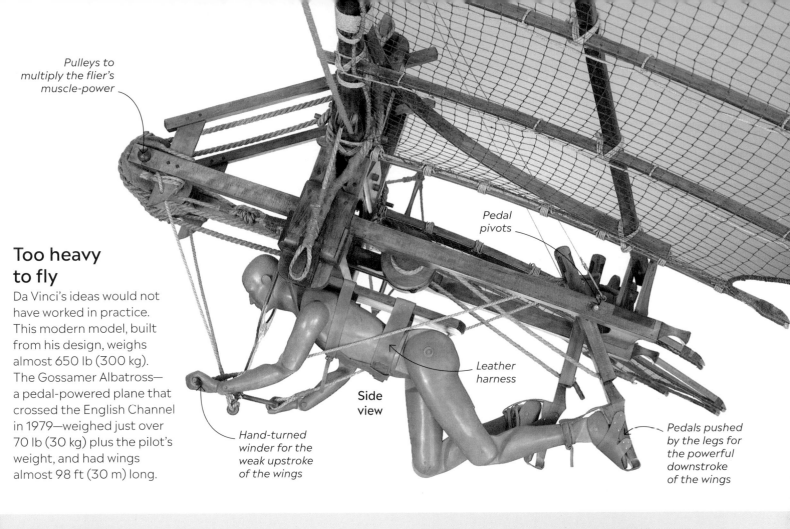

## Too heavy to fly

Da Vinci's ideas would not have worked in practice. This modern model, built from his design, weighs almost 650 lb (300 kg). The Gossamer Albatross—a pedal-powered plane that crossed the English Channel in 1979—weighed just over 70 lb (30 kg) plus the pilot's weight, and had wings almost 98 ft (30 m) long.

*Pulleys to multiply the flier's muscle-power*

*Pedal pivots*

*Leather harness*

Side view

*Hand-turned winder for the weak upstroke of the wings*

*Pedals pushed by the legs for the powerful downstroke of the wings*

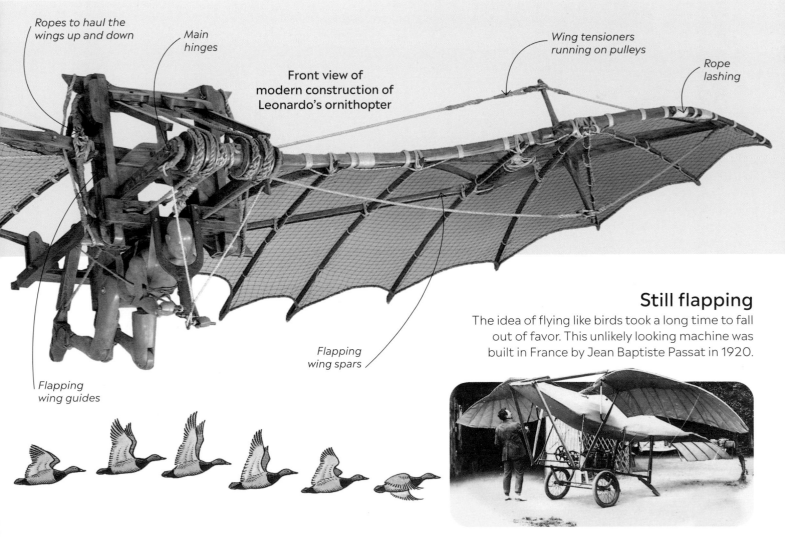

*Ropes to haul the wings up and down*

*Main hinges*

**Front view of modern construction of Leonardo's ornithopter**

*Wing tensioners running on pulleys*

*Rope lashing*

*Flapping wing guides*

*Flapping wing spars*

## Still flapping

The idea of flying like birds took a long time to fall out of favor. This unlikely looking machine was built in France by Jean Baptiste Passat in 1920.

# Lighter than air

The first human flights were not lifted by wings at all. In 1783, the Montgolfier brothers' huge cotton and paper balloon took off in Paris, France. It was filled with hot air, which is lighter than cold air. Ten days later, a rubberized silk balloon filled with a newly discovered gas called hydrogen flew even higher.

### The first flight
The Montgolfier brothers' balloon was filled with hot air and flown by Jean-François Pilâtre de Rozier and the Marquis d'Arlandes.

 **EYEWITNESS**

**Montgolfier brothers**
Joseph-Michel (left) and Jacques-Étienne Montgolfier (right) experimented with paper bags held upside-down over an open fire, calling the rising hot air that lifted them "Montgolfier gas." Before humans flew their balloon for the first time, a test flight carried a rooster, a duck, and a sheep!

### Early gas balloon
Unlike hot-air balloons, which cooled quickly, gas-powered flights lasted for hours. Gas balloonists used a control line to let out gas when they were ready to descend.

### Social climbing

In the late 19th century, ballooning became a fashionable society sport, and well-to-do people would compete for distance and height records.

### Fantastic!
More than 400,000 people witnessed the historic hydrogen balloon flight of Jacques Charles and Nicolas-Louis Robert, which is commemorated on this fan.

### Soft landing
Early balloons often carried wicker cushions strapped under the basket to absorb the blow of a heavy landing.

## Airships

In 1852, Henri Giffard made a cigar-shaped balloon, powered by a steam engine to make it "dirigible", or steerable. By the 1920s, "airships" with gas engines and rigid frames carried people across the Atlantic. But terrible fires caused by the flammable gas spelled the end for hydrogen airships.

### Dirigible milestone

In October 1910, the French-built Clément-Bayard II became the first dirigible to cross the English Channel.

### Zeppelins

Germany made the world's biggest airships. At 660 ft (200 m), World War I Zeppelins were three times longer than a modern jumbo jet.

## Riding high

Balloon races were popular in the late 1800s. Professional pilots would often ride the load ring to make room in the basket for joy-riding clients.

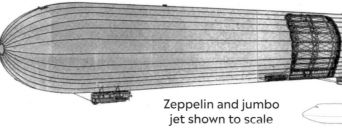

Zeppelin and jumbo jet shown to scale

## Up and down

Balloons carried extra weight, which they discarded to make up for gas seeping from the balloon. But dropping too much ballast made the balloon climb, forcing the pilot to release more gas. Early fliers carried pressure-controlled devices called statoscopes to show if their balloons were rising or falling.

Statoscope c.1900

Statoscope c.1870

Pocket barometer c.1909

## Making gas

Gas-powered balloons were filled with hydrogen gas, made by dripping sulfuric acid on iron turnings in contraptions like this.

## Gas detector

Hydrogen is very flammable, so it was vital to know if there were leaks. This meter detected its presence.

*Basket made of wicker for lightness and resistance to landing shocks*

*Anchor to tether the balloon during inflation*

# Gliding
# aloft

For a while, the future of flight seemed to be with lighter-than-air craft such as balloons. British engineer George Cayley thought otherwise. After many experiments with kite design, he created the world's first glider. Others followed, but controlling these flights proved difficult. In the 1890s a young German called Otto Lilienthal built a series of fragile hang glider-like craft that allowed him to make regular, controlled flights. This is why he is known as the "world's first true aviator."

*Tailplane*

### The oldest aircraft?
Kites were probably flown in China more than 3,000 years ago. They were developed in Europe in the 14th century.

### Learning to glide
Lilienthal studied each flying problem scientifically, analyzing problems and testing every solution critically. Aviators should learn to glide, he insisted, before taking the risky step of fitting a motor—advice that was crucial to the success of the Wright brothers (p.14).

 **EYEWITNESS**

**Sir George Cayley**
English inventor and engineer Sir George Cayley (1773–1857) was the first to understand how a wing works. Most modern aircraft are based on the kite-like model glider he made in 1804. In 1853, he built a full-size glider, which flew his terrified coachman across a small valley. It was the first recorded glider flight by a person.

### Plane ideas
George Cayley had many ideas for flying machines, including an airship and this person-carrying glider called a "governable parachute."

*Wing cover of unvarnished cotton*

**Otto Lilienthal had his own hill made near Berlin, so he could test and improve his gliders.**

Replica of Lilienthal's No.11 hang glider of 1895

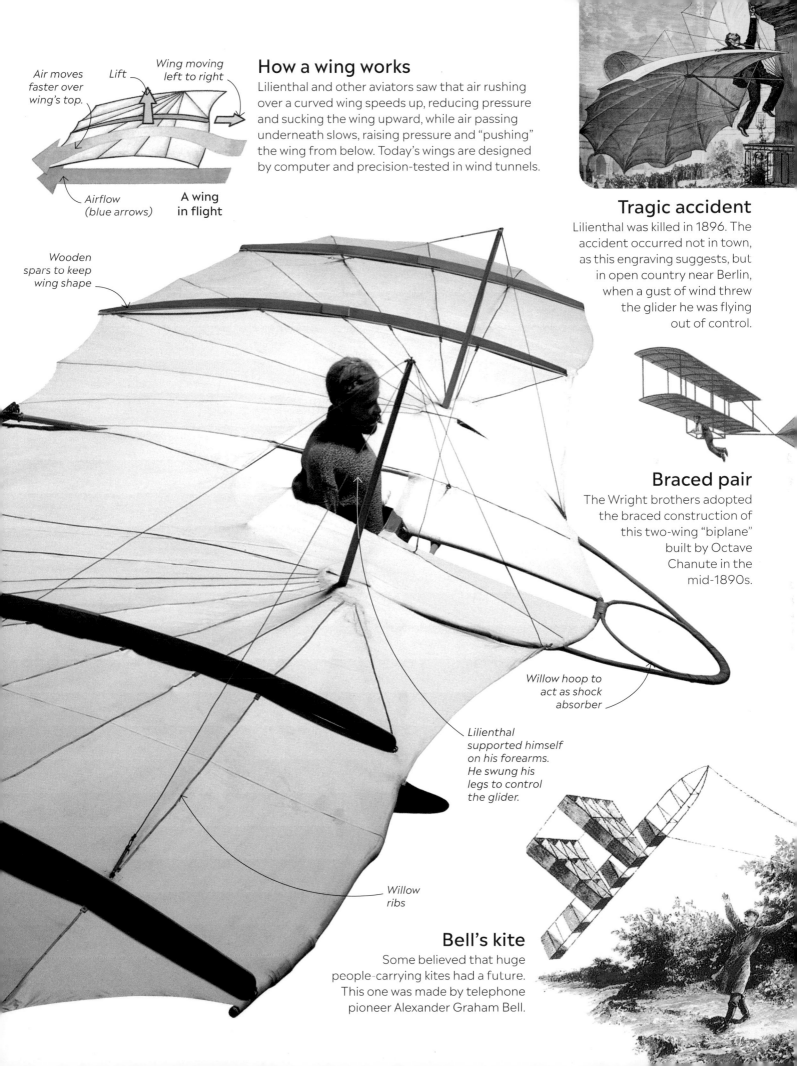

## How a wing works

Lilienthal and other aviators saw that air rushing over a curved wing speeds up, reducing pressure and sucking the wing upward, while air passing underneath slows, raising pressure and "pushing" the wing from below. Today's wings are designed by computer and precision-tested in wind tunnels.

Air moves faster over wing's top.

Lift

Wing moving left to right

Airflow (blue arrows)

A wing in flight

Wooden spars to keep wing shape

## Tragic accident

Lilienthal was killed in 1896. The accident occurred not in town, as this engraving suggests, but in open country near Berlin, when a gust of wind threw the glider he was flying out of control.

## Braced pair

The Wright brothers adopted the braced construction of this two-wing "biplane" built by Octave Chanute in the mid-1890s.

Willow hoop to act as shock absorber

Lilienthal supported himself on his forearms. He swung his legs to control the glider.

Willow ribs

## Bell's kite

Some believed that huge people-carrying kites had a future. This one was made by telephone pioneer Alexander Graham Bell.

# Powered flight

Gliders made brief winged flights possible, but to fly for any length of time, aircraft needed engines. In 1845, England's William Henson and John Stringfellow built a small working model of a plane, powered by a steam engine. It's not clear if it ever flew, but it opened the door to powered flight. By 1900, experts decided that steam engines were too heavy and focused on smaller, lighter, gas-powered engines.

### The gift of lift

People had long known that a little more than human power was needed to fly.

Silk-covered wings with 20 ft (6 m) span

"All-moving tailplane," or elevator

Wing-brace

Boiler

Drive pulley

Rudder

Steam tube

Connecting rod

### Steam power

Henson and Stringfellow built a lightweight steam engine for their model, with a boiler around 10 in (25 cm) long. A naphtha or alcohol burner boiled water, and steam rose through a row of conical tubes. This drove a piston, which turned a wooden drive pulley that spun the aircraft's two propellers.

Cylinder and piston

Henson and Stringfellow's steam engine

### Did it fly?

Stringfellow built another model in 1848 and launched it down a 30 ft (10 m) wire with the engine running. Some accounts say the model achieved powered flight by climbing a little in mid-air before it hit a wall.

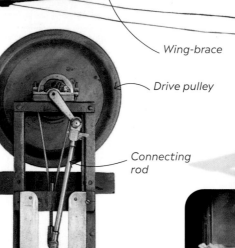

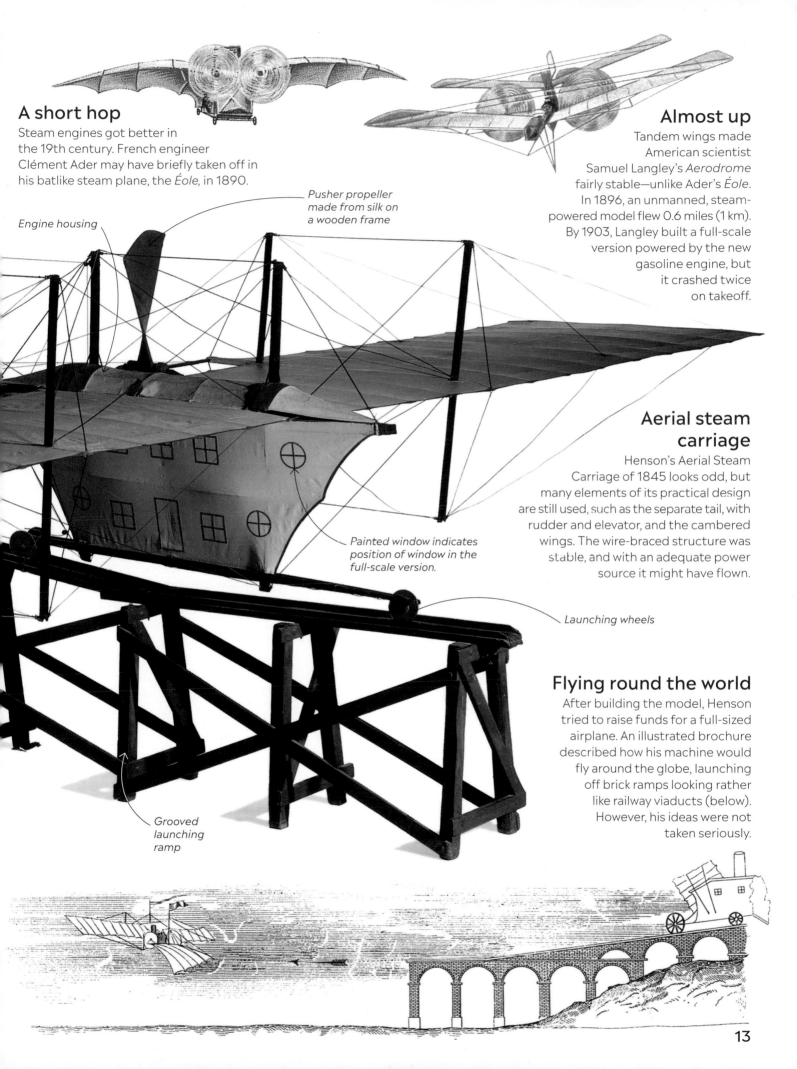

## A short hop

Steam engines got better in the 19th century. French engineer Clément Ader may have briefly taken off in his batlike steam plane, the *Éole,* in 1890.

## Almost up

Tandem wings made American scientist Samuel Langley's *Aerodrome* fairly stable—unlike Ader's *Éole.* In 1896, an unmanned, steam-powered model flew 0.6 miles (1 km). By 1903, Langley built a full-scale version powered by the new gasoline engine, but it crashed twice on takeoff.

*Engine housing*

*Pusher propeller made from silk on a wooden frame*

*Painted window indicates position of window in the full-scale version.*

*Launching wheels*

*Grooved launching ramp*

## Aerial steam carriage

Henson's Aerial Steam Carriage of 1845 looks odd, but many elements of its practical design are still used, such as the separate tail, with rudder and elevator, and the cambered wings. The wire-braced structure was stable, and with an adequate power source it might have flown.

## Flying round the world

After building the model, Henson tried to raise funds for a full-sized airplane. An illustrated brochure described how his machine would fly around the globe, launching off brick ramps looking rather like railway viaducts (below). However, his ideas were not taken seriously.

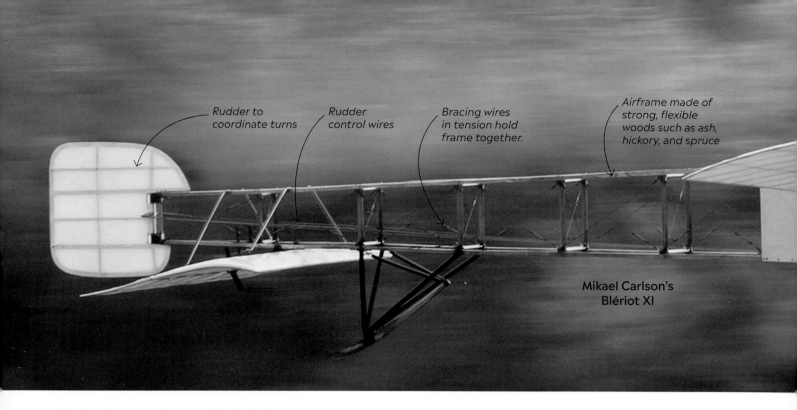

Rudder to coordinate turns

Rudder control wires

Bracing wires in tension hold frame together.

Airframe made of strong, flexible woods such as ash, hickory, and spruce

Mikael Carlson's Blériot XI

# The first airplanes

On December 17, 1903, at Kitty Hawk in the eastern US, a gas-powered flying machine built by brothers Orville and Wilbur Wright flew under control for a distance of 120 ft (36.5 m) before landing safely. It was the world's first powered, sustained, and controlled airplane flight. Progress was fast—in 1909, Frenchman Louis Blériot flew 26 miles (41 km) across the English Channel from France to England.

## The Wrights' *Flyer*

The Wright brothers realized that their plane needed some form of control to stop it rolling from side to side. So the *Flyer* had wires to warp (twist) the wings to lift one side or the other. This meant it could not only fly level but also make balanced, banked turns, rather like a bicycle cornering.

The Wrights' *Flyer* was **over four years** in the making—they began their experiments in 1899.

 **EYEWITNESS**

**Lilian Bland**
Born in 1878 in Kent, England, Bland became a sports journalist and photographer. In 1909, her uncle sent her a postcard of the Blériot XI, inspiring her to become the first woman to design, build, and fly her own aircraft, the *Mayfly*.

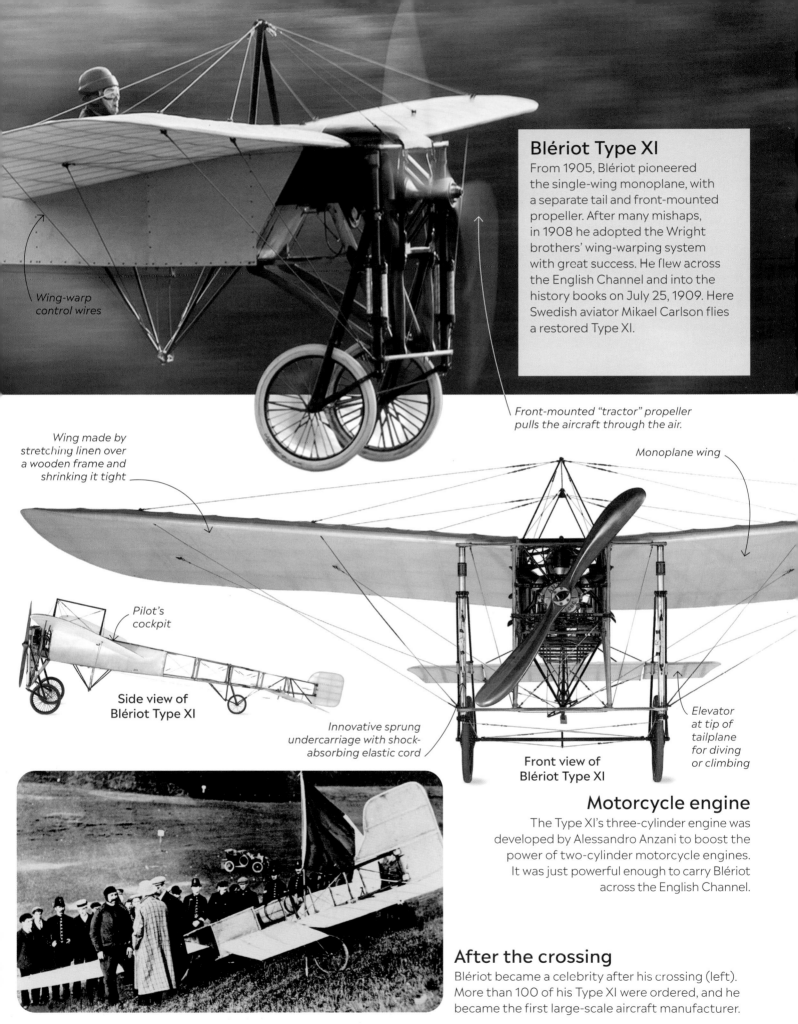

## Blériot Type XI

From 1905, Blériot pioneered the single-wing monoplane, with a separate tail and front-mounted propeller. After many mishaps, in 1908 he adopted the Wright brothers' wing-warping system with great success. He flew across the English Channel and into the history books on July 25, 1909. Here Swedish aviator Mikael Carlson flies a restored Type XI.

*Wing-warp control wires*

*Front-mounted "tractor" propeller pulls the aircraft through the air.*

*Monoplane wing*

*Wing made by stretching linen over a wooden frame and shrinking it tight*

*Pilot's cockpit*

**Side view of Blériot Type XI**

*Innovative sprung undercarriage with shock-absorbing elastic cord*

*Elevator at tip of tailplane for diving or climbing*

**Front view of Blériot Type XI**

## Motorcycle engine

The Type XI's three-cylinder engine was developed by Alessandro Anzani to boost the power of two-cylinder motorcycle engines. It was just powerful enough to carry Blériot across the English Channel.

## After the crossing

Blériot became a celebrity after his crossing (left). More than 100 of his Type XI were ordered, and he became the first large-scale aircraft manufacturer.

# Flying aces

The feats of the Wrights, Blériot, and other pilots turned aviation into a sensation. These early fliers deserved their fame, since planes were difficult to fly and accidents frequent. Sitting on an exposed seat was also uncomfortable and cold. When Blériot crossed the Channel, he wore a boiler suit, but special flying gear was soon developed.

Flying at 15,000 ft (4,500 m) or more, World War I pilots faced temperatures well **below freezing**, even on a warm day.

**Finding the way**
Pilots navigated by flying toward landmarks or following railway lines. Good maps were vital.

Pouch for maps

*Soft leather*

*Warm wool lining*

**Hot foot**
Warm boots were essential. These are soft, sheepskin-lined boots, originally thigh-length but cut down by the owner for convenience.

*Thick rubber sole gave good grip when climbing aboard the aircraft.*

## Flying gear c. 1916
World War I spurred the rapid development of flying gear. This selection was issued to British Royal Flying Corps pilots. Leather was initially thought the best material, but was soon replaced by one-piece Sidcot suits made of waxed cotton and lined with silk and fur.

*Goggle holders*

*Fold-up collar to keep neck warm*

### Head in the clouds
Cowl-type helmets with face masks were sometimes used for high-altitude flying. But some air aces felt more alert without a helmet or goggles.

### Goggle-eyed
Goggles gave protection against the wind. This pair is tinted to reduce glare and is made with shatter-resistant glass.

*Button-up cuffs to keep out wind*

*Leather gloves lined with sheepskin mitten*

### Windproof
High speeds and long flights in World War I meant suits had to be more windproof at the neck, wrists, and ankles.

### Hands in the air
Stuck out in the airstream on the controls, hands could suffer frostbite if not protected by warm gloves.

# Double wings

The earliest airplanes had one, two, three, or more sets of wings. Blériot's cross-Channel flight in 1909 (pp.14–15) made single-wing monoplanes popular, but while fast, their long, slender wings were fragile and accident-prone. At the start of World War I (1914–1918), most fighter planes and observation aircraft were the slower but safer double-winged biplanes. However, rapid technical advances during the war transformed aviation.

*Radiator for engine-cooling water*

*Wooden propeller*

## Fokker Triplane
Some triplanes (with three sets of wings) were built during the war. The German wartime Fokker Triplane was "fearsome to look at and climbs like a lift [elevator]." It was also highly maneuverable. But aerodynamic drag slowed triplanes down, and they fell out of use after 1918.

In 1912, the British and French army commanders **banned monoplanes**, considering them dangerous and unreliable.

*Light wire-spoked landing wheels*

## IMMELMANN TURN

The "dogfights" (aerial duels) of World War I showed how maneuverable airplanes had become. The Immelmann Turn, named after the German flying ace Max Immelmann, was a very steep climbing turn that allowed pilots to evade pursuit or mount a hit-and-run attack.

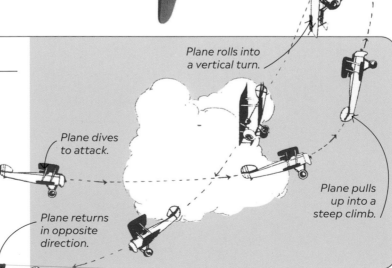

*Plane rolls into a vertical turn.*

*Plane dives to attack.*

*Plane pulls up into a steep climb.*

*Plane returns in opposite direction.*

Timer to ensure gun fires through the propeller when the blades are horizontal.

8-cylinder 300-hp Hispano-Suiza "V" engine

Vickers forward-firing machine gun aimed through a hole in the radiator.

Throttle controls speed of engine.

Pilot's seat

Rudder bar

Fuel tank

Ash frame

Bracing struts

Lower wing centre section

## Fighting like dogs

Single-seat planes with forward-firing machine guns took part in "dogfights." Since the pilot had to aim the whole aircraft at the enemy, flying skill was vital.

## Bristol Fighter (c.1917)

Early in the war, hazardous artillery spotting and observation were performed by slow two-seaters, often protected by faster single-seaters. When the British Bristol Fighter came on the scene in 1917, however, its powerful engine made it fast enough to act as both spotter and fighter.

*Continued on next page* **19**

Continued from previous page

## Bristol Fighter

Struts linking upper and lower wing

Bracing wires

Lewis machine-gun on Scarff swivel ring lets the observer fire in many directions.

Fuselage longerons made of straight-grained spruce

Observer's position

## Doped up

The wooden wing frames looked flimsy, but were stronger when covered in linen that was shrunk into place, and then painted with "cellulose dope."

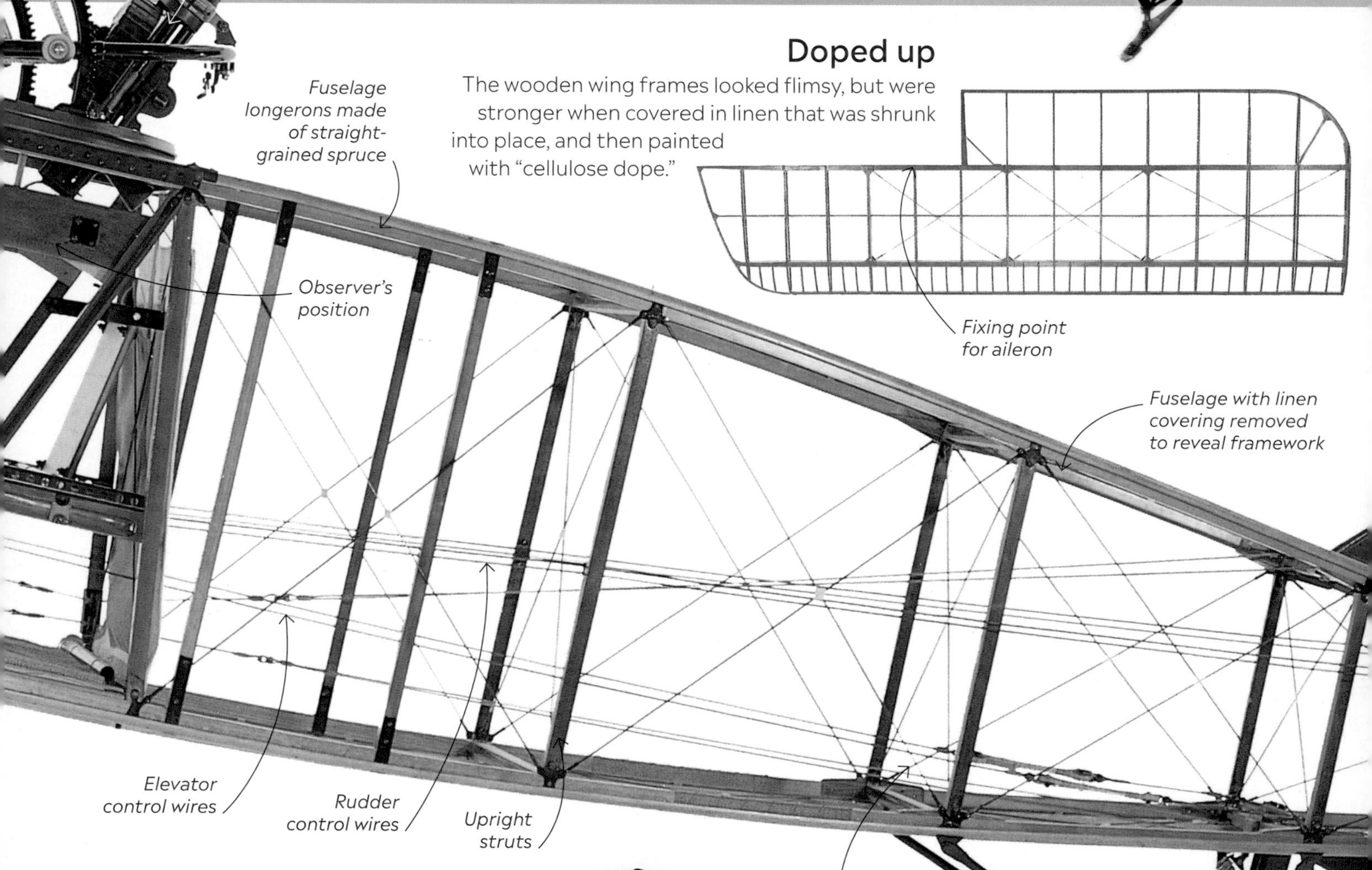

Fixing point for aileron

Fuselage with linen covering removed to reveal framework

Elevator control wires

Rudder control wires

Upright struts

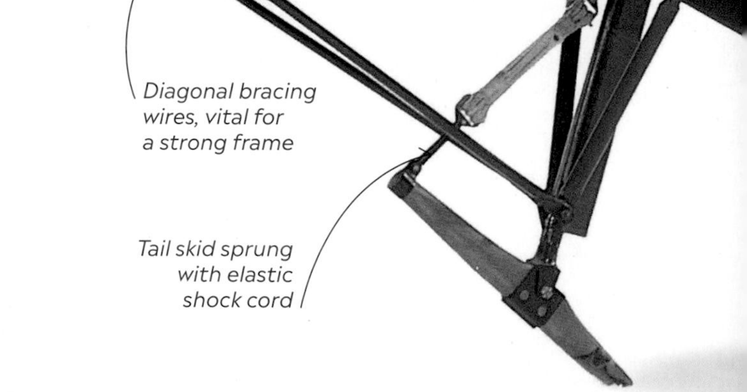

Diagonal bracing wires, vital for a strong frame

Tail skid sprung with elastic shock cord

### 👁 EYEWITNESS

**Sabiha Gökçen**
Born in 1913, Sabiha Gökçen became the world's first female fighter pilot in 1937. Female pilots were not allowed to participate in combat missions at the time, but with the support of her adoptive father, the President of Turkey Mustafa Kemal Atatürk, Gökçen took part in 32 military operations.

## What a drag

Biplanes had a large frontal area. This meant that they suffered from considerable drag. Even though the Bristol Fighter had a powerful engine, it could still only reach about 120 mph (180 kph).

## All tied up

Biplane wings were held in alignment by struts, rather like the rungs in a ladder. They were also braced with wires to cope with the forces of flying.

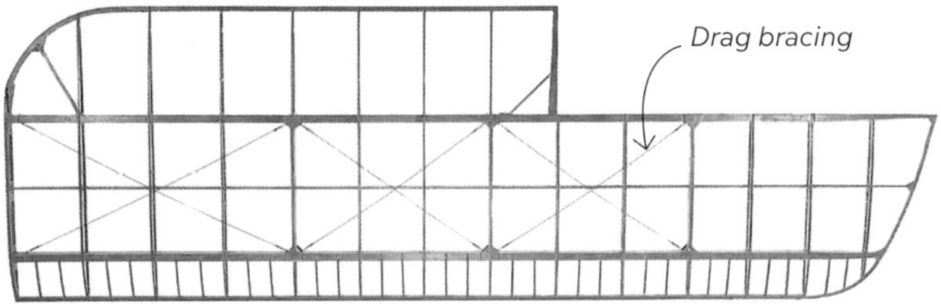

Drag bracing

Wing frame

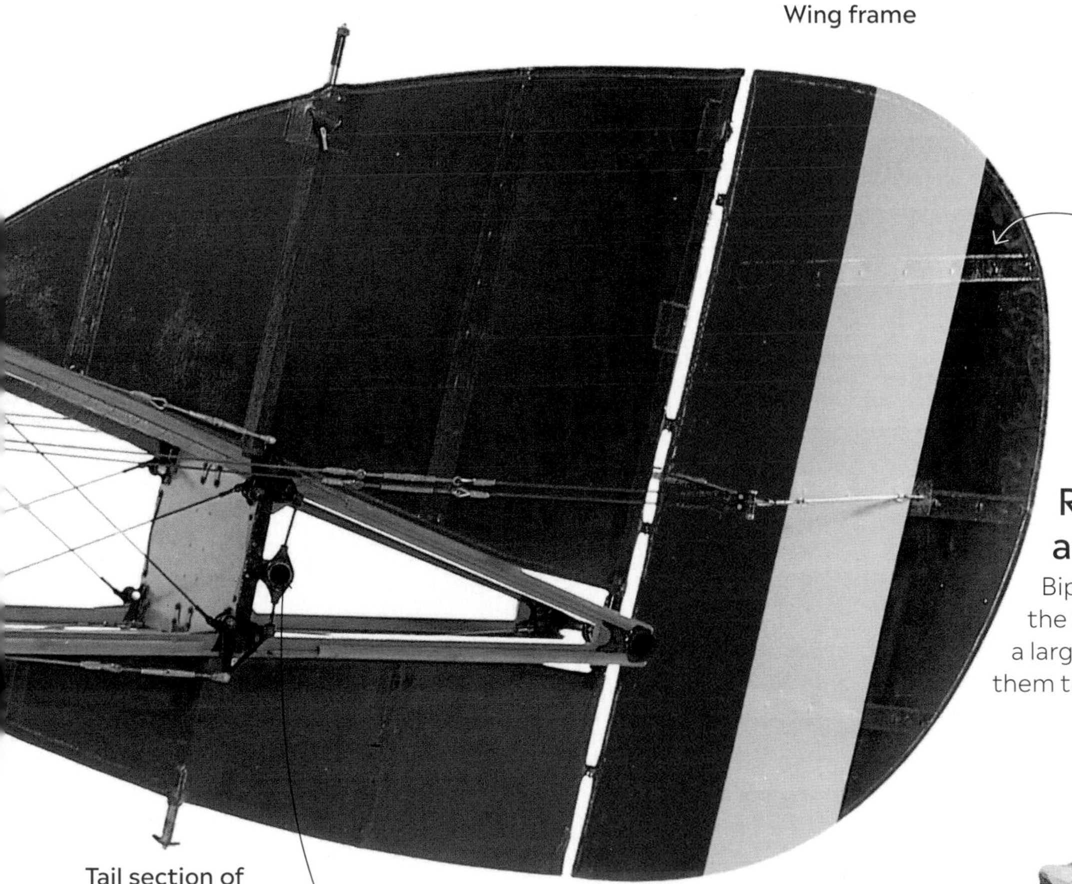

Rudder

## From bombs to people

Large biplane bombers built at the end of World War I were the basis for the first airliners in peacetime.

## Rudder authority

Biplanes such as the Bristol Fighter had a large rudder to help them turn accurately.

Tail section of Bristol Fighter

Support for tailplane

## Flying boats

Ever larger planes were built after World War I. This Short S.14 Sarafand flying boat (1932) could stay aloft for 11 hours.

# The evolving plane

At the first international airshow in Reims, France, in August 1909, none of the flimsy, wood-frame aircraft could fly faster than 47 mph (75 kph) or climb higher than 500 ft (150 m). Within four years, aircraft were flying at more than 120 mph (200 kph) at heights of up to 20,000 ft (6,000 m). By 1929, streamlined all-metal planes were hurtling across the sky at speeds unimaginable 20 years earlier.

### Deperdussin 1909

This French company was a leading aircraft manufacturer before World War I, setting many speed records. This example shows various typical pre-war features—wing-warping lateral control (p.14), a low-powered engine, and extensive wire bracing.

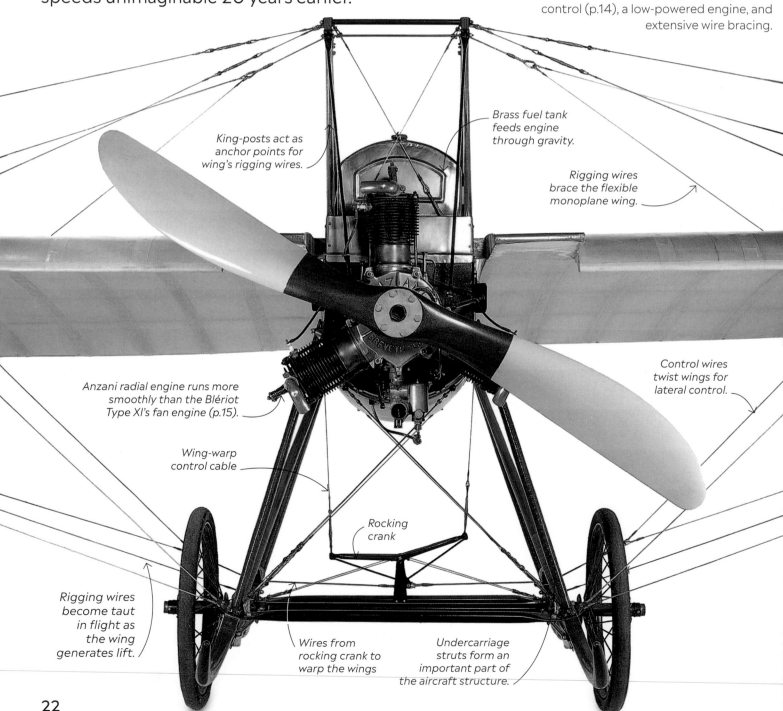

King-posts act as anchor points for wing's rigging wires.

Brass fuel tank feeds engine through gravity.

Rigging wires brace the flexible monoplane wing.

Anzani radial engine runs more smoothly than the Blériot Type XI's fan engine (p.15).

Control wires twist wings for lateral control.

Wing-warp control cable

Rocking crank

Rigging wires become taut in flight as the wing generates lift.

Wires from rocking crank to warp the wings

Undercarriage struts form an important part of the aircraft structure.

## Sopwith Pup 1917

By World War I, lightweight rotary engines (pp.28–29) were propelling fighters like this Sopwith Pup to 115 mph (185 kph) or more, and improved control allowed planes to engage in dogfights. Pilots no longer twisted the wings to bank the plane but raised or lowered hinged flaps, called ailerons, on rigid wings (p.41). Toward the end of the war, plane makers began to experiment with sleek, strong, metal-skinned fuselages.

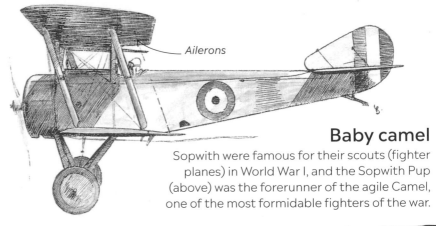

*Ailerons*

### Baby camel

Sopwith were famous for their scouts (fighter planes) in World War I, and the Sopwith Pup (above) was the forerunner of the agile Camel, one of the most formidable fighters of the war.

*Gunsight*

*Vickers machine gun*

*Aluminum cowling catches the oil thrown out by a rotary engine.*

*Streamlined struts*

*100-hp Gnome rotary engine*

*Efficient cambered wing*

*Bracing wires strengthen the aircraft's structure, essential for dogfights*

**In August 1917, a Sopwith Pup became the first plane to land on a moving ship, the HMS *Furious*.**

*Exhaust slot*

*Continued on next page*

23

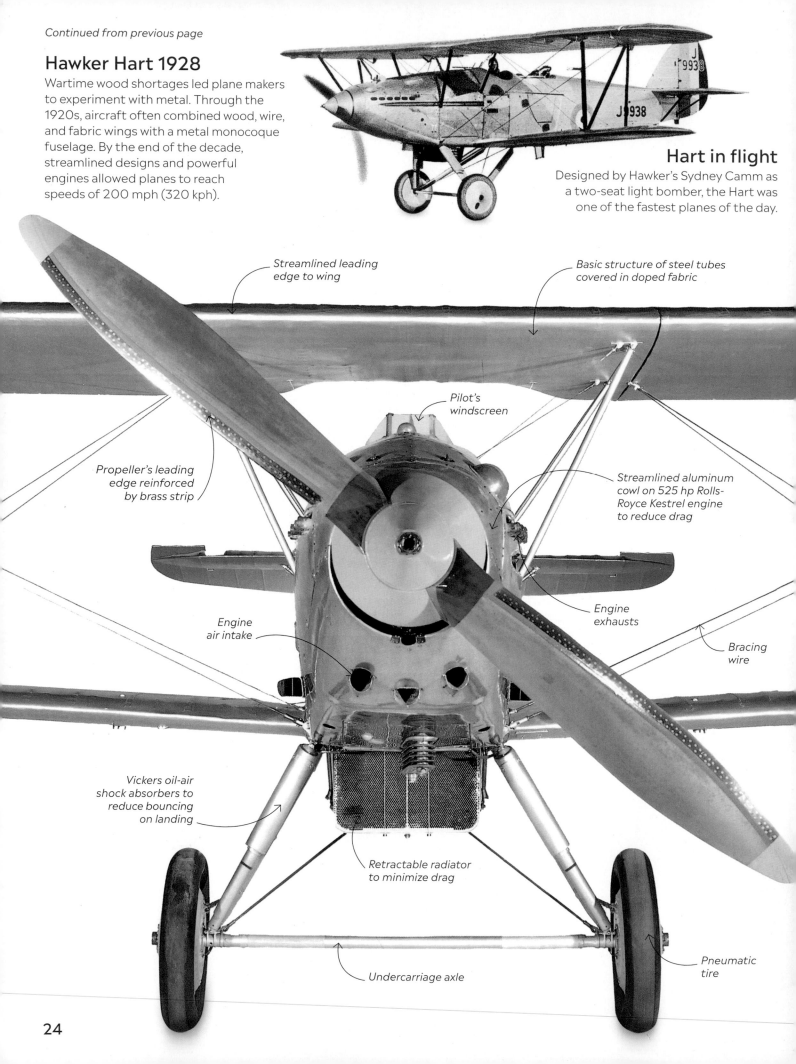

## Hawker Hart 1928

*Continued from previous page*

Wartime wood shortages led plane makers to experiment with metal. Through the 1920s, aircraft often combined wood, wire, and fabric wings with a metal monocoque fuselage. By the end of the decade, streamlined designs and powerful engines allowed planes to reach speeds of 200 mph (320 kph).

### Hart in flight
Designed by Hawker's Sydney Camm as a two-seat light bomber, the Hart was one of the fastest planes of the day.

Streamlined leading edge to wing

Basic structure of steel tubes covered in doped fabric

Propeller's leading edge reinforced by brass strip

Pilot's windscreen

Streamlined aluminum cowl on 525 hp Rolls-Royce Kestrel engine to reduce drag

Engine exhausts

Bracing wire

Engine air intake

Vickers oil-air shock absorbers to reduce bouncing on landing

Retractable radiator to minimize drag

Pneumatic tire

Undercarriage axle

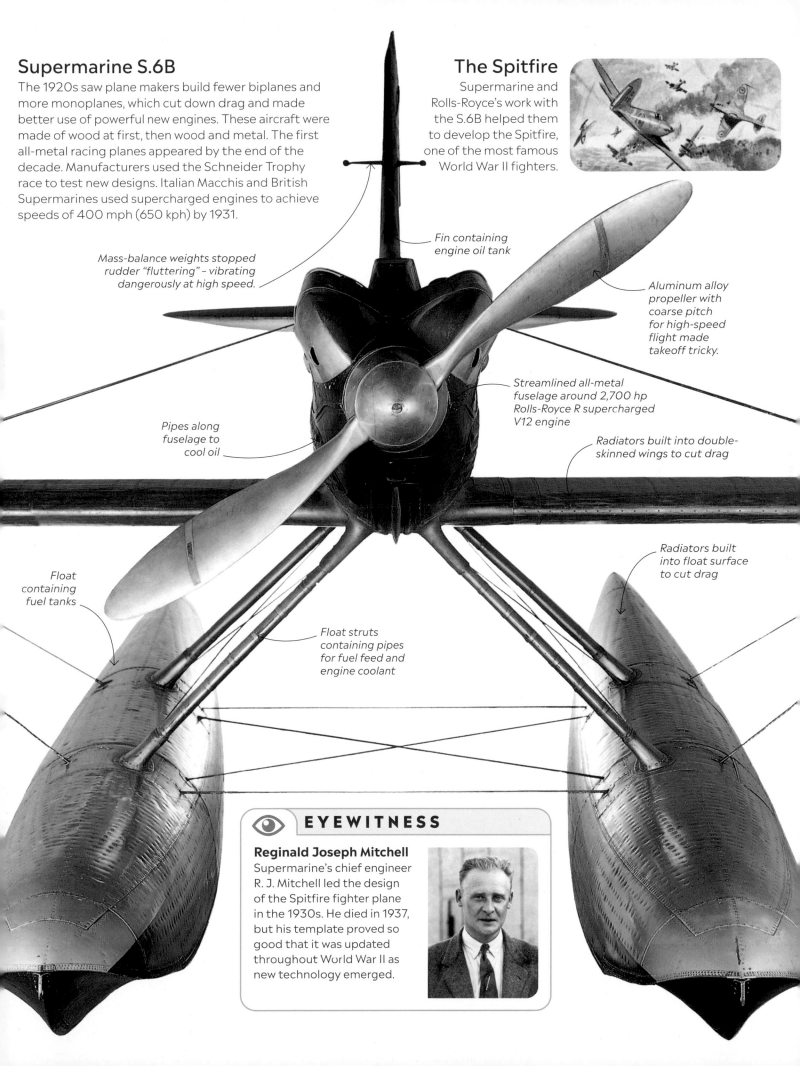

# Supermarine S.6B

The 1920s saw plane makers build fewer biplanes and more monoplanes, which cut down drag and made better use of powerful new engines. These aircraft were made of wood at first, then wood and metal. The first all-metal racing planes appeared by the end of the decade. Manufacturers used the Schneider Trophy race to test new designs. Italian Macchis and British Supermarines used supercharged engines to achieve speeds of 400 mph (650 kph) by 1931.

# The Spitfire

Supermarine and Rolls-Royce's work with the S.6B helped them to develop the Spitfire, one of the most famous World War II fighters.

*Fin containing engine oil tank*

*Mass-balance weights stopped rudder "fluttering" – vibrating dangerously at high speed.*

*Aluminum alloy propeller with coarse pitch for high-speed flight made takeoff tricky.*

*Pipes along fuselage to cool oil*

*Streamlined all-metal fuselage around 2,700 hp Rolls-Royce R supercharged V12 engine*

*Radiators built into double-skinned wings to cut drag*

*Radiators built into float surface to cut drag*

*Float containing fuel tanks*

*Float struts containing pipes for fuel feed and engine coolant*

# Light aircraft

Today's single-engined light airplanes work in much the same way as early aircraft, with aluminum alloys and polyester composites replacing the traditional wood or steel-tube frame. They usually have a fixed undercarriage, a monoplane wing, a simple fuselage and tail, and a small gas or diesel engine to turn the propeller.

### Epic flight

Perhaps the most famous light plane is the Ryan NYP *Spirit of St. Louis*, in which Charles Lindbergh flew solo across the Atlantic in 1927.

*Variable-pitch propeller gives shorter takeoff and fast cruise.*

### High-tech tourer

Cirrus's SR20 and SR22 were the first planes of their type to feature advanced flight displays instead of traditional instrument dials.

*Cabin seats four or five people in comfort.*

*Fluid flow from porous metal leading edge deices the wing.*

### Cirrus SR22

Cirrus Aircraft launched the SR series of high-performance piston-engine light aircraft in the late 1990s. Lightweight materials and advanced technology have made the SR22 very popular among private owners. Nevertheless, traditional all-metal aircraft built by Cessna and Piper remain popular with flight training organizations.

*Wings and fuselage made entirely from composite (reinforced polyester) material*

## Plane and simple

The all-metal Cessna 172E Skyhawk is the classic all-purpose light plane used for training, leisure, and business. More than 45,000 have been built since 1955.

## Little racer

The basic layout for light planes—high wings, engine in the nose, and fixed wheels—was set in the 1930s, when this Comper Swift racing plane was built.

## Cirrus Vision SF50 Jet

Built from carbon fiber composite material and billed as "the world's first single-engine personal jet," this aircraft can carry up to seven people at 358 mph (576 kph).

**Cirrus SR22** has a **parachute** that brings the **whole plane safely down** to Earth in emergencies.

*Wide doors on both sides for easy cabin access*

*Automatic variable-pitch propeller gives best thrust for throttle setting.*

*Turbocharged 315 hp air-cooled six cylinder engine*

*Efficiently shaped propeller blades fitted with deicing system to prevent snow and ice build-up*

# Aero-engines

Powered flight only became possible with the creation of piston engines for cars in the early 20th century. Finding water-cooled car engines heavy and air-cooled motorcycle engines apt to cut out mid-flight, aviators started to make their own light, powerful, and ever more sophisticated models. Only after World War II did the developing jet engine replace piston engines for most large aircraft.

## Cool jacket

To save weight, some water-cooled aero-engines, such as this one from c. 1910, had thin copper water jackets electrically coated onto the cylinders.

*Exhaust*

*Carburetor*

*Copper cooling jacket around the cylinder*

## Vital spark

Spark plugs ignite the fuel charge to drive the piston down in each engine cylinder.

*Pipe to carry fuel and air mixture from the carburetor to the cylinders*

*Cylinder cut away to reveal piston*

*Piston—driven down by burning fuel and up by the rotating crankshaft*

*Lightweight, cast-aluminum alloy crankcase*

*Flange for exhaust pipe*

*Cast-iron cylinders with fins to improve cooling by increasing the area of metal exposed to the airflow*

## Wheels to wings

Like many early aero-engines, this 1910 Anzani "fan" type engine (with the cylinders spread out in a fan shape) came from a motorcycle. This was the kind of engine used by Blériot for his Channel crossing in 1909 (pp.14–15).

*Carburetor mixes fuel and air at the required rate.*

*Float controls level of fuel in the carburetor.*

*Propeller mounting*

## Rotary engine

The Séguin brothers' rotary engine, first used in 1909, spun around with the propeller to cool the cylinders, but the spinning mass was hard to control. By the 1920s, conventional engines had improved enough to combat overheating.

*Stationary crankshaft: the whole engine spins around this.*

*Inlet pipes channel the fuel–air mix from crankcase to cylinders.*

*Valves let fuel in and burned gases (exhaust) out.*

*Cylinders cooled by passing air as they rotate*

*Crankcase rotates with the cylinders.*

*Finely machined cylinders with light, thin walls only 0.04 in (1 mm) thick*

*Connecting rods to pistons are all joined to a single bearing around the crankshaft.*

## Aero-giant

Bridging the gap between piston engines and jets, the Saunders-Roe Princess flying boat was powered by 10 Bristol Proteus turboprop engines (p.36).

*Direct fuel injection replaces carburetor.*

*Turbocharger forces more air into the engine to increase power.*

## More power

This impressive Rotax 916 iS/c engine weighs 189 lb (85.8 kg), but produces 160 hp—more than four times the power of Blériot's 150 lb (70 kg) Anzani of 1908.

# The propeller

Propellers are like spinning wings, thrusting the plane forward in the same way as wings lift it up. Propeller shape is as crucial to performance as wing shape, and the evolution of propeller design has dramatically improved efficiency. Propellers have become stronger, too, changing from layers of wood called laminations to aluminum and carbon composites, to cope with the increasing power of aero-engines.

## Wright 1909

The Wright brothers were the first to understand how a propeller works and to calculate the thrust it produced.

## Phillips 1893

Designed by early English aviator Horatio Phillips and looking like a ship's screw, this propeller was intended to drive a 400 lb (180 kg) aircraft.

*Propeller blade made from strips of wood*

*Blade angle (pitch) is steeper and closer to the hub.*

*Tip travels farther and faster than hub.*

*Propeller rotates this way.*

*Hub*

*Leading edge*

*Trailing edge*

## Paragon 1909

This blade's experimental shape was not necessary, given the slow spinning speeds of the time.

## Pitch and twist

The thrust developed by a propeller varies with its speed and the angle at which its blades carve through the air—its pitch. Because a propeller's tip spins faster than its hub, the blade must be twisted in order to keep thrust even along its length.

*Brass cover to protect the blade from sea spray*

## Lang 1917
Long and robust, this laminated propeller was made to cope with the power of a 225-hp Sunbeam engine on a Short 184 seaplane.

## Wotan 1917
This elegant German propeller was made by gluing laminations together and then carving them to form a smoothly tapered aerofoil.

## Extra blades
As engine power increased, propellers were made with three, four, or more blades to cope with the extra load.

*Laminations of spruce and ash*

*Piston and links to vary blade pitch (angle)*

## Hele-Shaw Beacham 1928
By the late 1920s, aircraft used variable-pitch propellers where the angle of the blades could be changed to suit the conditions.

*Variable-pitch blade gives the right pitch for takeoff and high-speed cruising.*

## Fairey-Reed 1922
Aircraft designers wanted thin blades that cut easily through the air to make their planes faster. Thin wood blades are weak, so from 1920 strong, thin propellers were made from forged aluminum.

## Integrale 1919
The brass sheath covering this wooden-bladed propeller was designed to protect it from enemy attack.

## Three-blade Hartzell Scimitar
"Scimitar" blades, such as those fitted to this Hartzell three-blade variable-pitch propeller, are a recent development. Their aerodynamically refined shape maximizes cruise performance while reducing noise.

## Hardy travelers

Early passenger planes were tiny. The 1934 de Havilland Dragon Rapide carried eight passengers; the "big" Boeing 247D held 10. Passengers rode in loose wicker chairs until fixed rows of seats became standard in the 1930s. Before pressurized cabins, planes either flew low, often in turbulence, or high, where some passengers suffered bitter cold and altitude sickness.

# Flying the world

The time between the two world wars was the heroic age of aviation—the era of the first nonstop crossing of the Atlantic by Alcock and Brown (p.42), Lindbergh's solo crossing (p.26), and Australian Charles Kingsford Smith's epic Pacific flight in 1928. Airlines formed, and more people experienced the speed and novelty of flying. In 1933, Boeing launched the 247, the world's first modern airliner.

### Stars in the sky

Air travel was glamorous and new. Many early passengers on the London to Paris route were American film stars or sports celebrities.

### Flying boat to Egypt

Flying boats let people fly to far-flung places. The ability to land on water helped where airports were few and far between.

### Croydon airport

The world's first modern airport buildings were built at Croydon, near London, England, in 1928.

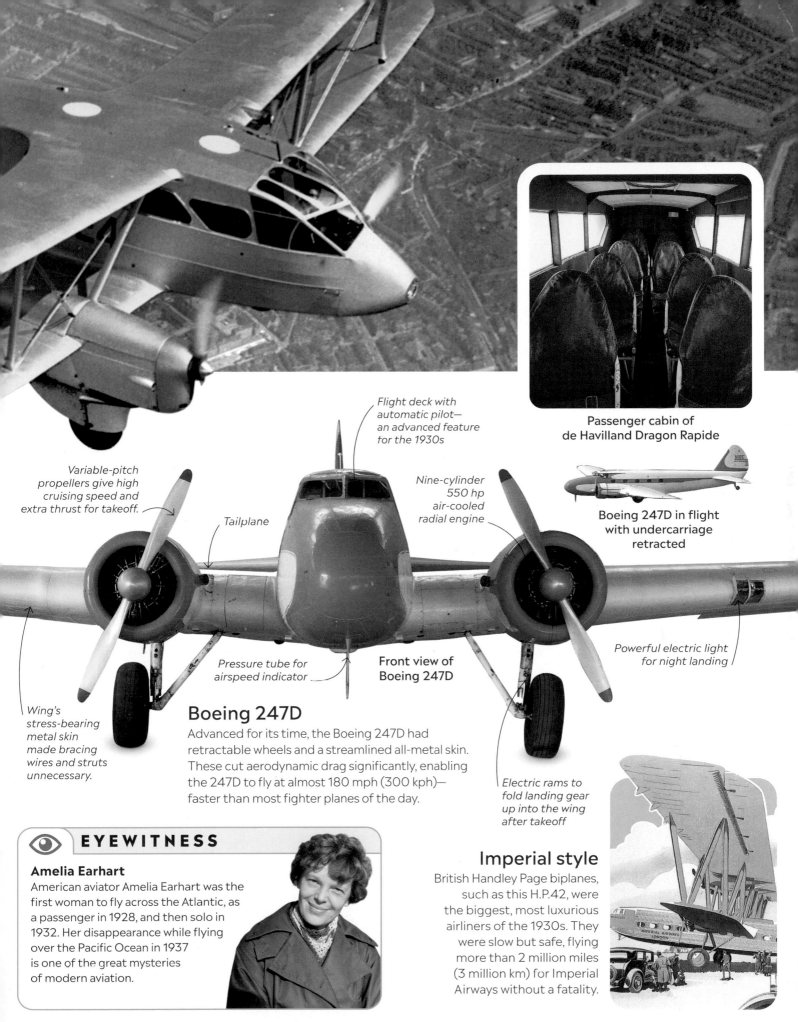

Passenger cabin of
de Havilland Dragon Rapide

Flight deck with
automatic pilot—
an advanced feature
for the 1930s

Variable-pitch
propellers give high
cruising speed and
extra thrust for takeoff.

Nine-cylinder
550 hp
air-cooled
radial engine

Boeing 247D in flight
with undercarriage
retracted

Tailplane

Pressure tube for
airspeed indicator

Front view of
Boeing 247D

Powerful electric light
for night landing

Wing's
stress-bearing
metal skin
made bracing
wires and struts
unnecessary.

## Boeing 247D

Advanced for its time, the Boeing 247D had
retractable wheels and a streamlined all-metal skin.
These cut aerodynamic drag significantly, enabling
the 247D to fly at almost 180 mph (300 kph)—
faster than most fighter planes of the day.

Electric rams to
fold landing gear
up into the wing
after takeoff

### EYEWITNESS

**Amelia Earhart**
American aviator Amelia Earhart was the
first woman to fly across the Atlantic, as
a passenger in 1928, and then solo in
1932. Her disappearance while flying
over the Pacific Ocean in 1937
is one of the great mysteries
of modern aviation.

## Imperial style

British Handley Page biplanes,
such as this H.P.42, were
the biggest, most luxurious
airliners of the 1930s. They
were slow but safe, flying
more than 2 million miles
(3 million km) for Imperial
Airways without a fatality.

# The jet age

## De Havilland Comet

The world's first jetliner entered service in 1952, halving international flight times, but early versions suffered catastrophic failures.

Before the 1950s, only the wealthy could afford to fly. The first jet airliners paved the way for mass transport, with millions of people able to travel quickly and safely around the world. The latest aircraft are faster, quieter, and safer than ever, with sophisticated electronic control systems, streamlined lightweight frames, and quieter turbofan engines.

## Boeing 707

The age of jet travel really began with the Boeing 707, introduced in 1958. It set the template for modern airliners with swept (backward-angled) wings and engines suspended on pylons.

## Faster than a bullet

Concorde was a supersonic airliner flown between 1976 and 2003. It could cross the Atlantic Ocean in only 3½ hours, traveling at 1,350 mph (2,170 kph) – twice the speed of sound.

*Winglets help smooth airflow to reduce drag.*

*It typically takes 950 gal (4,330 l) of paint to cover the plane.*

*Fuel tanks in the elevators are filled or drained to help balance the aircraft.*

*Emergency doors allow passengers to escape quickly using inflatable slides.*

## Mass travel

Built in response to the famous Boeing 747 "jumbo jet," the Airbus A380 is a giant of the skies. With a wingspan of 261 ft (80 m) it is able to carry up to 853 passengers and weighs around 634 tons (575 metric tons) on takeoff.

## Modern airliners

New construction methods using materials such as carbon fiber have made aircraft much more efficient. This means they can fly further, with the longest nonstop route now covering the 9,527 miles (15,332 km) between New York and Singapore in about 19 hours.

## Air traffic control

Around 90,000 commercial flights take off and land every day around the world. Air traffic controllers keep everyone safe by ensuring aircraft don't fly too close together. At the busiest airports, a plane lands every 90 seconds.

## In the future

Manufacturers are exploring new technology to make aircraft more efficient and kinder to the environment. The Airbus ZEROe concept aircraft uses a blended-wing body and hybrid hydrogen-fueled turbofan engines.

## Modern airports

Airports handle millons of passengers and huge amounts of cargo every year. The busiest airport in the world is currently Hartsfield-Jackson Atlanta International Airport, with 94 million passengers in 2022.

**Boeing 747s have carried over**
# 5.6 billion people
**around the world since 1970.**

*At takeoff, the engines produce the same power as around 2,500 family cars.*

*Each A380 is made from around 4 million individual parts.*

# Jet propulsion

The invention of the jet engine in the 1930s was revolutionary. Jet-powered fighters, introduced near the end of World War II, immediately beat the best piston fighters' top speeds of around 440 mph (700 kph). By the 1960s, even commercial jet airliners were faster. Today, military jets can easily fly at over 1,200 mph (2,000 kph) and airliners travel nonstop from New York to Singapore.

*Rolls-Royce Trent 1000 jet engine from a Boeing 787, with panels opened up*

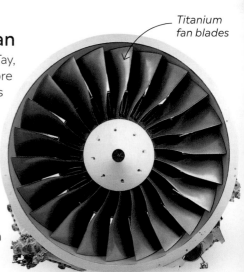

*Cone smooths jet flow to produce most efficient thrust.*

*Sawtooth blades around fan housing minimize noise.*

## TURBOJET AND TURBOFAN

The first turbojets produced thrust from their high-energy exhaust gas. They are less efficient than turbofans, which also use the lower-speed airflow from a turbine-driven fan.

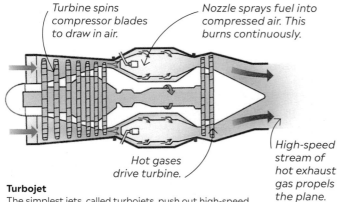

*Turbine spins compressor blades to draw in air.*

*Nozzle sprays fuel into compressed air. This burns continuously.*

*Hot gases drive turbine.*

*High-speed stream of hot exhaust gas propels the plane.*

**Turbojet**
The simplest jets, called turbojets, push out high-speed exhaust gases to propel the aircraft. Turbojets powered Concorde and are still used in fast military planes.

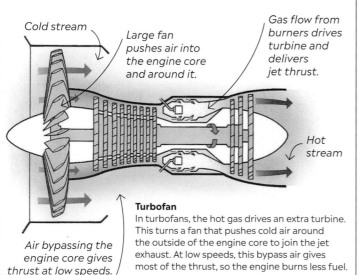

*Cold stream*

*Large fan pushes air into the engine core and around it.*

*Gas flow from burners drives turbine and delivers jet thrust.*

*Hot stream*

*Air bypassing the engine core gives thrust at low speeds.*

**Turbofan**
In turbofans, the hot gas drives an extra turbine. This turns a fan that pushes cold air around the outside of the engine core to join the jet exhaust. At low speeds, this bypass air gives most of the thrust, so the engine burns less fuel.

## Breaking the "sound barrier"

In 1947, US Air Force pilot Chuck Yeager flew the specially built Bell X-1 rocket plane faster than the speed of sound—around 700 mph (1,100 kph).

## Power fan

In the Rolls-Royce Tay, the fan pushes more than three times as much air through the bypass duct to provide propulsion as through the engine core. In earlier turbofans, the proportions were about equal. This improves both fuel economy and power.

*Titanium fan blades*

**Front view of Rolls-Royce Tay**

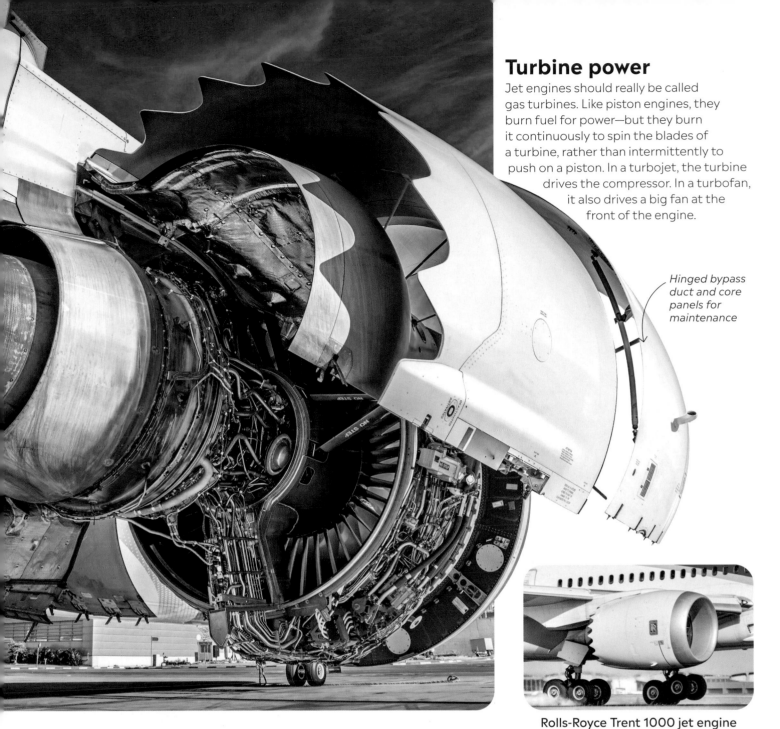

## Turbine power

Jet engines should really be called gas turbines. Like piston engines, they burn fuel for power—but they burn it continuously to spin the blades of a turbine, rather than intermittently to push on a piston. In a turbojet, the turbine drives the compressor. In a turbofan, it also drives a big fan at the front of the engine.

*Hinged bypass duct and core panels for maintenance*

Rolls-Royce Trent 1000 jet engine

### Blowing hot and cold

More than two-thirds of a turbofan's power comes from the stream of cold air through the bypass duct. Exhaust nozzles mix this with the hot stream from the engine to reduce noise.

*Exit for cold stream bypass*

**Rear view of Rolls-Royce Tay**

*Exit for hot stream from engine core*

# Landing gear

Early airplanes had narrow, wire-spoked wheels mounted on fragile struts with rubber-cord suspension. With heavier planes and higher speeds came more complex "undercarriages" with pressed-steel wheels and "oleos" (fluid-cushioned landing legs). By the 1940s, most undercarriages folded up (retracted) into the wings to reduce air resistance. The jet age further increased demands on landing gear, leading to innovations such as disc brakes and anti-skid systems. Modern jetliners' complex suspension and braking systems help 150-ton airplanes land at 125 mph (200 kph) or more and stop quickly and safely.

## Landing on water
In the early days of aviation there were few good landing strips, so it made sense to land on water. A step two-thirds of the way along their underside helped seaplanes to rise up from the water during takeoff.

## Lightly spoked
There were no brakes on this wheel from a pre-World War I plane. Because of this, it did not need elaborate crisscrossed spokes to resist braking forces.

*Rubber shock absorbers*

*Wooden landing strut*

*Skid to prevent tipping forward when landing on soft ground*

## Sprung tail-skid
Lightweight early planes used a simple tail-skid instead of a rear wheel for landing.

## Coming down gently
The 1909 Deperdussin came down so lightly and slowly that rubber straps could absorb the impact. Curved skids on the front helped stop the plane from pitching forward on landing.

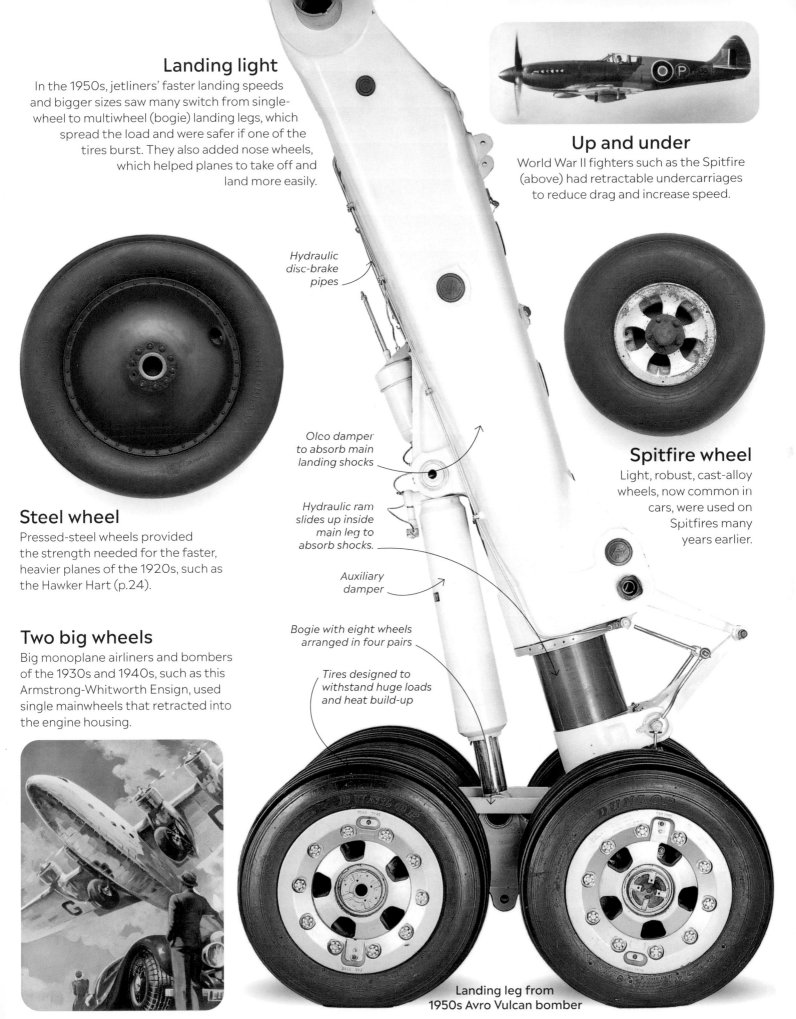

## Landing light

In the 1950s, jetliners' faster landing speeds and bigger sizes saw many switch from single-wheel to multiwheel (bogie) landing legs, which spread the load and were safer if one of the tires burst. They also added nose wheels, which helped planes to take off and land more easily.

## Up and under

World War II fighters such as the Spitfire (above) had retractable undercarriages to reduce drag and increase speed.

Hydraulic disc-brake pipes

## Steel wheel

Pressed-steel wheels provided the strength needed for the faster, heavier planes of the 1920s, such as the Hawker Hart (p.24).

Olco damper to absorb main landing shocks

Hydraulic ram slides up inside main leg to absorb shocks.

## Spitfire wheel

Light, robust, cast-alloy wheels, now common in cars, were used on Spitfires many years earlier.

Auxiliary damper

## Two big wheels

Big monoplane airliners and bombers of the 1930s and 1940s, such as this Armstrong-Whitworth Ensign, used single mainwheels that retracted into the engine housing.

Bogie with eight wheels arranged in four pairs

Tires designed to withstand huge loads and heat build-up

Landing leg from
1950s Avro Vulcan bomber

# Controlling the plane

An airplane is controlled in three dimensions. It can pitch nose up or nose down to climb or dive, roll to either side using flaps on the wings, or yaw to the left or right using the rudder. Pilots use all three controls simultaneously, and must constantly adjust them to keep the plane flying straight and level.

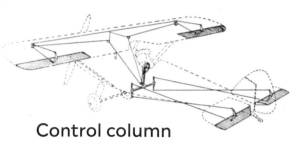

### Control column
The idea of a single lever, linked to the elevators and ailerons, to control both pitch and roll, was pioneered by Blériot (pp.14–15).

### Rudder bar
Pushing the rudder bar with either foot swings the rudder left or right to control yaw.

*Main wing meets the air at a sharper angle, increasing lift.*

*Nose comes up.*

*Elevators raised, air pushing the tail down*

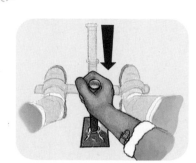

### Pitching up
Pulling the control column back raises the elevators. The plane's nose rises and the wing meets the air at a greater angle, increasing lift.

*Elevators flat, keeping the plane level*

### Level flight
In level flight, the tail helps to keep the plane steady, like the flights on a dart. If the aircraft is pitched up or down by turbulence, the tailplane helps to keep it level.

*Main wing meets the air at a shallower angle, reducing lift and drag.*

*Nose dips.*

*Elevators lowered, increasing tail lift*

### Pitching down
Lowering the elevators, by pushing the control column forward, makes the tailplane lift, and pitches the nose downward. The aircraft gathers speed as it descends, so the pilot must reduce power for a gentle landing.

## Rolling left

Moving the control column left raises the aileron on the left wing, reducing lift on that side, and lowers the right aileron.

*Right aileron lowered, increasing lift on right wing*

*Left aileron raised, reducing lift on left wing*

## Rolling right

Moving the control column right raises the right aileron and lowers the left. Once the plane is at the correct angle, the pilot centers the column to prevent further roll.

*Left aileron lowered, increasing lift on left wing*

*Right aileron raised, reducing lift on right wing*

## Turning left

While moving on the ground, pushing the rudder to the left makes the plane yaw the same way. In mid-air, the plane makes a banked turn, like cornering on a bicycle. To do this, the pilot must roll and yaw the plane at the same time: for a left turn, they push both the control column and the rudder left.

*Rudder swung left, yawing the plane to the left*

## Turning right

To bank right, the pilot presses the control column and the rudder to the right. Balancing the two controls to achieve just the right bank angle requires skill and experience.

*Rudder swung right, yawing the plane to the right*

## Aerial twists

Mastering the flight controls allowed daring maneuvers, either in aerial combat or, from the 1920s, in "flying circuses" that thrilled crowds with breathtaking aerobatics in agile biplanes.

# In the cockpit

Before closed cockpits were developed in the 1920s, pilots suffered howling winds, freezing cold, and damp. Early cockpits had just a few instruments, plus the basic controls—a throttle to adjust engine speed, a rudder bar at the pilot's feet, and a control column, or joystick, between the knees. This simple setup is still used in light planes today.

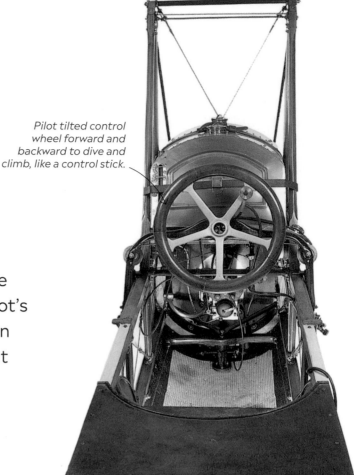

*Pilot tilted control wheel forward and backward to dive and climb, like a control stick.*

## Deperdussin 1909

Early cockpits had no instruments and a fuel tank blocked the view, so pilots constantly had to lean out to check altitude and pitch.

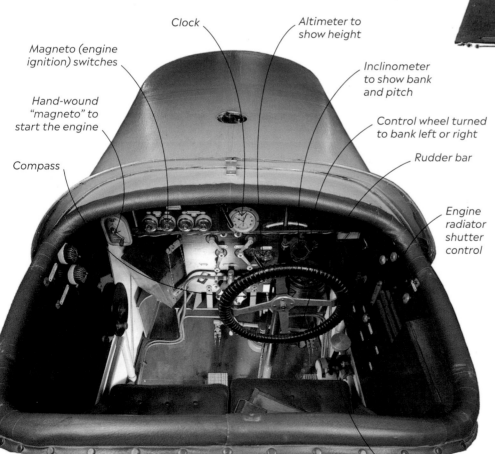

Magneto (engine ignition) switches

Hand-wound "magneto" to start the engine

Compass

Clock

Altimeter to show height

Inclinometer to show bank and pitch

Control wheel turned to bank left or right

Rudder bar

Engine radiator shutter control

Engine throttle and fuel mixture controls

## Vickers Vimy 1919

The Vimy flew long-range bombing raids over Germany at the end of World War I, with a pilot and an observer seated side by side. The pilot had to read the engine speed and oil pressure directly from gauges on the wing-mounted engines!

 **EYEWITNESS**

On June 14–15, 1919, British aviators John Alcock (pilot, left) and Arthur Brown (navigator, right) made the first nonstop Atlantic crossing by an airplane, flying a converted Vickers Vimy bomber. After enduring freezing fog and drizzle during 16 hours in the air, they nosed-over on landing in an Irish bog.

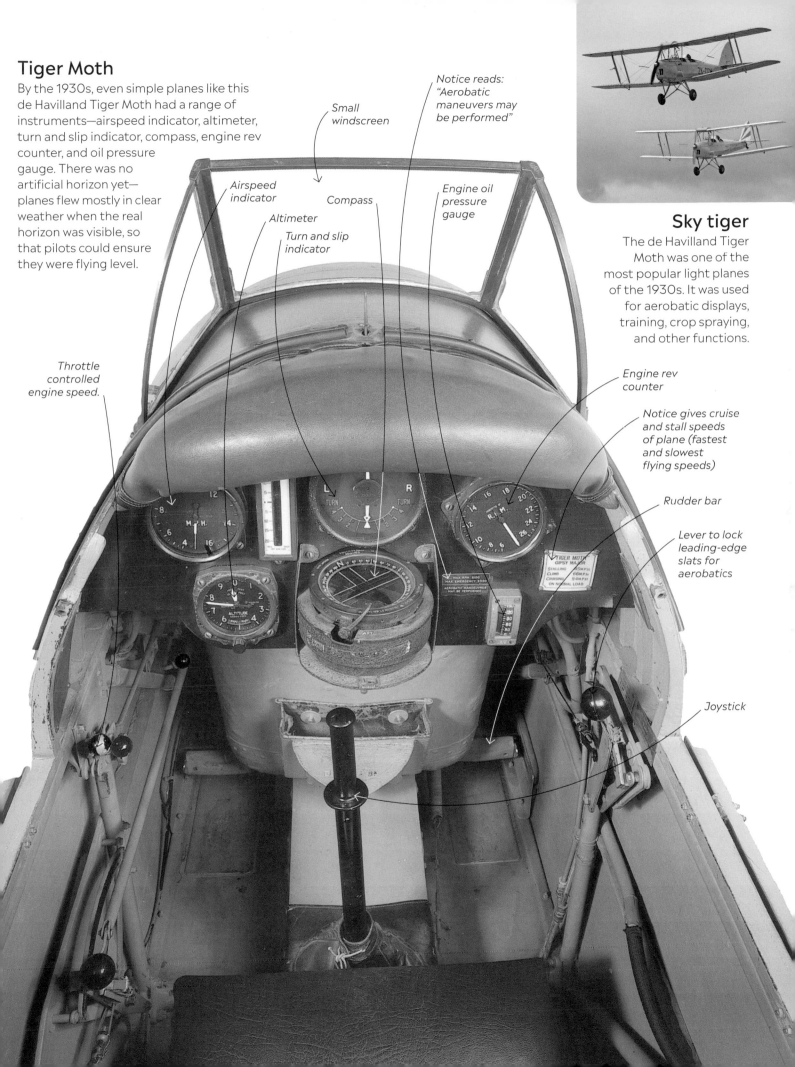

## Tiger Moth

By the 1930s, even simple planes like this de Havilland Tiger Moth had a range of instruments—airspeed indicator, altimeter, turn and slip indicator, compass, engine rev counter, and oil pressure gauge. There was no artificial horizon yet—planes flew mostly in clear weather when the real horizon was visible, so that pilots could ensure they were flying level.

Small windscreen

Notice reads: "Aerobatic maneuvers may be performed"

Airspeed indicator

Altimeter

Turn and slip indicator

Compass

Engine oil pressure gauge

Throttle controlled engine speed.

### Sky tiger

The de Havilland Tiger Moth was one of the most popular light planes of the 1930s. It was used for aerobatic displays, training, crop spraying, and other functions.

Engine rev counter

Notice gives cruise and stall speeds of plane (fastest and slowest flying speeds)

Rudder bar

Lever to lock leading-edge slats for aerobatics

Joystick

# On the
# flight deck

The flight deck of a modern jetliner looks dauntingly complicated with its array of electronic displays and switches for things such as engine condition, hydraulics, and navigational aids, not to mention the basic flight controls. The dials of older aircraft have largely been replaced by computer screens.

**Modern airliners are increasingly automated, using computer-based "fly-by-wire" systems.**

Overhead panel

Master warning light

Master caution light

Navigation display

Primary flight display

Throttle levers to control engine power

Captain's side

Air vent

Radio dial to speak to Air Traffic Control

Rudder pedals

## Glass cockpit

In a glass cockpit, the many analog dials of old aircraft are combined in electronic screens. The most important screens are the primary flight display (showing data from all the flight instruments) and navigation display (showing compass, radar screen, and map functions). Pilots can customize their displays and toggle between different views.

### Modern Cockpits

In modern aircraft such as this Airbus, the cockpit offers a wealth of data. The four main flight instruments are the airspeed indicator, altimeter (height above sea level), artificial horizon, and direction indicator. Most planes also have turn-and-slip and vertical speed indicators. Engine instruments show temperature, pressure, power, fuel level, and more.

*Autopilot controls*

*Engine data and warnings display*

*Landing gear indicator and automatic brake selector panel*

*Stopwatch start/stop button*

*Undercarriage control lever*

*Standby display unit*

### First officer's (copilot's) side

*Flight-management and guidance system control and display unit*

*Sidestick for "fly-by-wire" flight controls*

# Flying
# instruments

Early aviators flew with very few instruments. The dangers of stalling by flying too slow soon made accurate airspeed indicators essential. Altimeters and compasses became standard too, but it took until 1929, when Elmer Sperry developed gyroscope-stabilized instruments, to give pilots enough information to fly safely. Gyroscopes—a kind of spinning top that stays level at any angle—let pilots "fly on instruments" when visibility was poor.

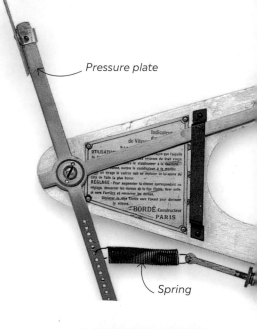

Pressure plate

Spring

## Double tube

This is one of the first reliable airspeed indicators. It used two pipes to compare the pressure difference between normal "static" air pressure and the "dynamic" air pressure caused by the speed of the aircraft.

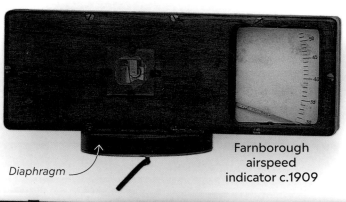

Diaphragm

Farnborough airspeed indicator c.1909

## How fast?

Using an anemometer (wind meter), pilots worked out their speed by noting how often the device's fan turned in a period of time measured on a stopwatch.

Static pipe

Static tube

Dynamic pipe

Dynamic tube

Pitot head

## Mach meter

Introduced in the 1950s, this device shows how fast a plane is flying relative to the speed of sound.

## Pitot head

The Farnborough-style airspeed indicator was refined over time into a device called a pitot head, which was fixed to the airframe and linked by tubes to a gauge in the cockpit.

Connecting tube

Gauge

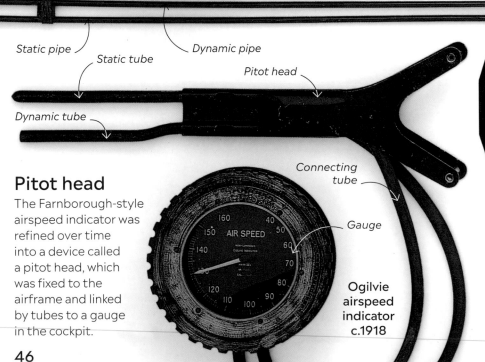

Ogilvie airspeed indicator c.1918

## Airspeed indicator

After World War II, speed indicators usually had a red line to show the maximum safe speed of a plane.

## Wing spring

Here, airspeed is shown by how far the pressure plate is forced back against a spring by the airflow.

## How straight?

The pointer indicates turn rate and the ball in the tube tells pilots if they needs to add rudder to a turn.

## Which way?

This "flight director" helps pilots follow radio beams that guide them in to land.

With the sighting string below the horizon, the plane is diving.

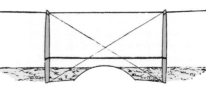

With the sighting string above the horizon, the plane is climbing.

## How high?

By World War I, large cockpit-mounted altimeters had replaced small handheld devices such as the one to the right.

With the sighting string dipping right below the horizon, the plane is rolling right.

## On the level?

Early pilots could only use the horizon to see if they were pitching or rolling, perhaps using a sighting string (above). After 1929, gyroscopic artificial horizons allowed them to check their orientation at night or in thick clouds.

## Inside a black box

All modern airliners and military planes carry a "black box" flight data recorder. The box (which isn't always black) records what happens during the flight, monitoring flight deck instruments, engine data, and even what the crew says.

Flight data recorder

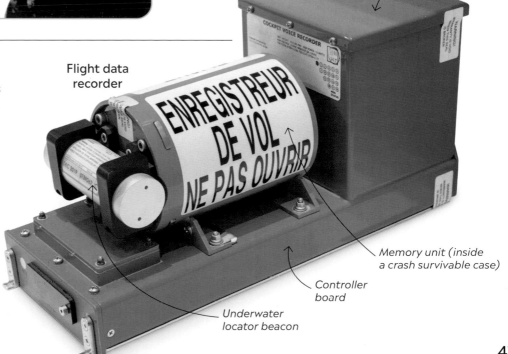

*Power supply*

*Memory unit (inside a crash survivable case)*

*Controller board*

*Underwater locator beacon*

### Boxed in

Flight data was once recorded on magnetic tape stored inside a titanium alloy case. Data is now stored on memory chips.

# Rotating wings

The concept of flying machines with rotating wings dates back to at least the 1400s. The invention of the autogyro by Spain's Juan de la Cierva in the 1920s showed that this type of craft was practical. A benefit of rotary-wing aircraft over airplanes was that they would not stall when flying at low speed.

## Juan de la Cierva

Cierva believed rotary-wing aircraft would make flying safer.

*Rotor blade*

## Autogyro

Early inventors used engines to turn the rotors of their helicopter-like machines directly, but Cierva saw that rotating wings could provide lift without an engine. Like a sycamore pod whirling gently down to Earth, a rotating wing spins by itself, pushed by the pressure of air on its underside. Cierva called this self-rotation, or autogyro in Spanish. A forward-facing propeller provided airspeed to keep the rotor spinning.

### Cierva C-30

C-30s like this one were used in World War II for military reconnaissance and other roles.

*Tailplane angled up on this side to counterbalance the blades' rotation*

*Fabric-covered steel-tube fuselage similar to that of a 1920s biplane*

K4232

*Steerable tail wheel*

### Cars of the sky

Autogyro makers such as America's Pitcairn company in the 1930s tried to market their aircraft as the Model T Ford of the sky—without the inconvenience of getting stuck in traffic jams.

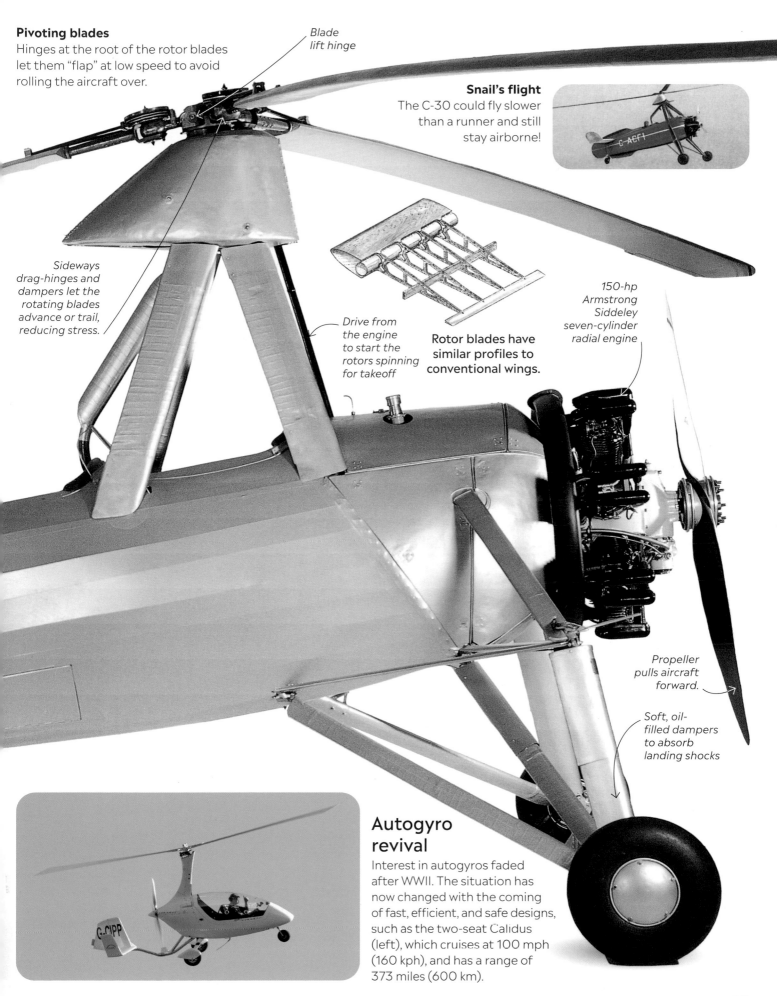

**Pivoting blades**
Hinges at the root of the rotor blades let them "flap" at low speed to avoid rolling the aircraft over.

Blade lift hinge

**Snail's flight**
The C-30 could fly slower than a runner and still stay airborne!

*Sideways drag-hinges and dampers let the rotating blades advance or trail, reducing stress.*

*Drive from the engine to start the rotors spinning for takeoff*

**Rotor blades have similar profiles to conventional wings.**

*150-hp Armstrong Siddeley seven-cylinder radial engine*

*Propeller pulls aircraft forward.*

*Soft, oil-filled dampers to absorb landing shocks*

## Autogyro revival

Interest in autogyros faded after WWII. The situation has now changed with the coming of fast, efficient, and safe designs, such as the two-seat Calidus (left), which cruises at 100 mph (160 kph), and has a range of 373 miles (600 km).

# Helicopter

Helicopters are more versatile than airplanes—they can climb and descend vertically, hover, and land in confined spaces. They are also more complicated, using an additional flight control—the collective pitch lever that commands upward and downward motion. This requires additional piloting skill, but the helicopter's adaptability still makes it an incredibly useful aircraft.

Rotor blades

## Spinning dreams
Early helicopter "designs" were highly impractical.

Pitch controls

Instrument panel

## HOW A HELICOPTER FLIES

Like an autogyro (p.48), a helicopter's rotor blades act as rotating wings. However, because the rotor is driven by an engine, the spinning forces make the helicopter body turn in the opposite direction. This "torque reaction" makes the aircraft unstable. A tail rotor balances this force, and also serves as a rudder to move the tail left or right.

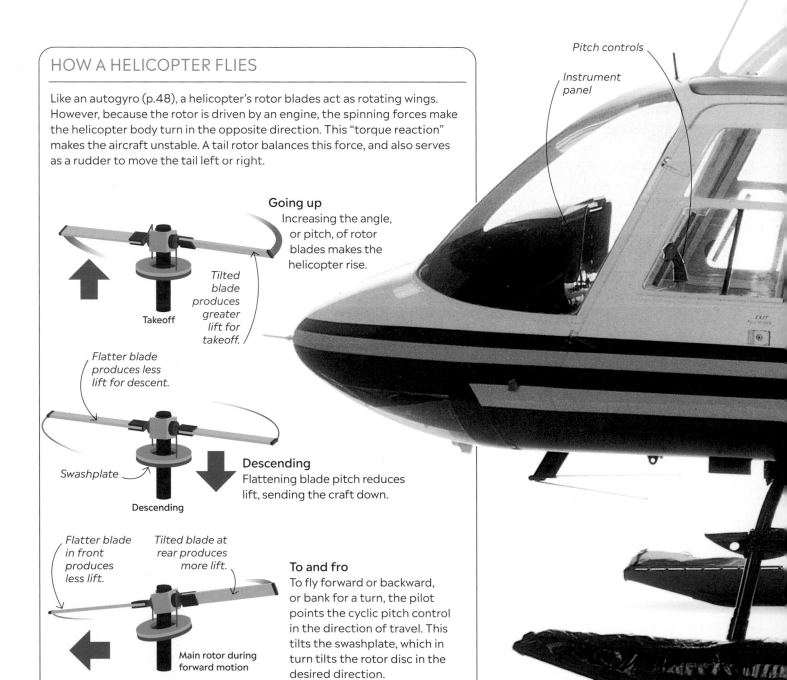

**Going up**
Increasing the angle, or pitch, of rotor blades makes the helicopter rise.

*Tilted blade produces greater lift for takeoff.*

Takeoff

*Flatter blade produces less lift for descent.*

*Swashplate*

Descending

**Descending**
Flattening blade pitch reduces lift, sending the craft down.

*Flatter blade in front produces less lift.*

*Tilted blade at rear produces more lift.*

**To and fro**
To fly forward or backward, or bank for a turn, the pilot points the cyclic pitch control in the direction of travel. This tilts the swashplate, which in turn tilts the rotor disc in the desired direction.

Main rotor during forward motion

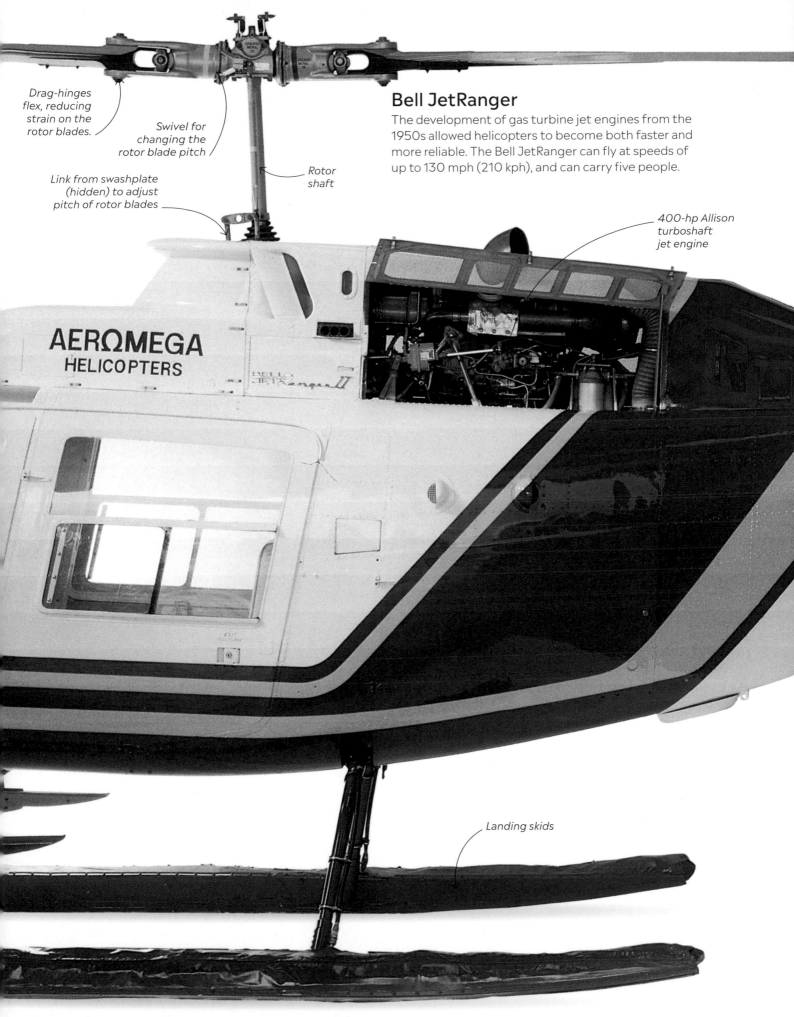

Drag-hinges flex, reducing strain on the rotor blades.

Swivel for changing the rotor blade pitch

Link from swashplate (hidden) to adjust pitch of rotor blades

Rotor shaft

## Bell JetRanger

The development of gas turbine jet engines from the 1950s allowed helicopters to become both faster and more reliable. The Bell JetRanger can fly at speeds of up to 130 mph (210 kph), and can carry five people.

400-hp Allison turboshaft jet engine

AERΩMEGA
HELICOPTERS

Landing skids

Continued on next page

Continued from previous page

## Clipper of the clouds

In the 19th century, inventors dreamed up ideas for rotary-wing flying machines. George Cayley (p.10) made model helicopters, while French visionary Gabriel de la Landelle conceived the majestic Steam Airliner (left) in 1863.

## The first helicopter flight?

In 1907, just four years after the Wright brothers' first flight, this primitive tandem-rotor helicopter, built by French mechanic Paul Cornu, lifted him clear of the ground for 20 seconds. Practical helicopters would not emerge until the late 1930s.

*Pitch stabilizers*

*Tail boom*

*Swashplate*

*Rotor blade pitch control rods*

*Leading edge of rotor blade*

*Steel tube fuselage covered in fabric*

**British Royal Air Force Sikorsky R-4**

*Boom*

*Pilot's seat*

## The birth of the helicopter

Building stable helicopters proved difficult until the invention of the autogyro (pp.48–49) showed how to control direction by altering the angle of the rotor blades. Germany's Henrich Focke built a helicopter-like craft in 1937, improved upon by Anton Flettner a few months later. But it was Igor Sikorsky's VS-300 (below) from 1939 that created the basic helicopter template still in use today.

*Air-cooled radial engine*

*Tail wheel*

**Sikorsky VS-300**

## Military use

The helicopter's ability to reach inaccessible places is invaluable in war.

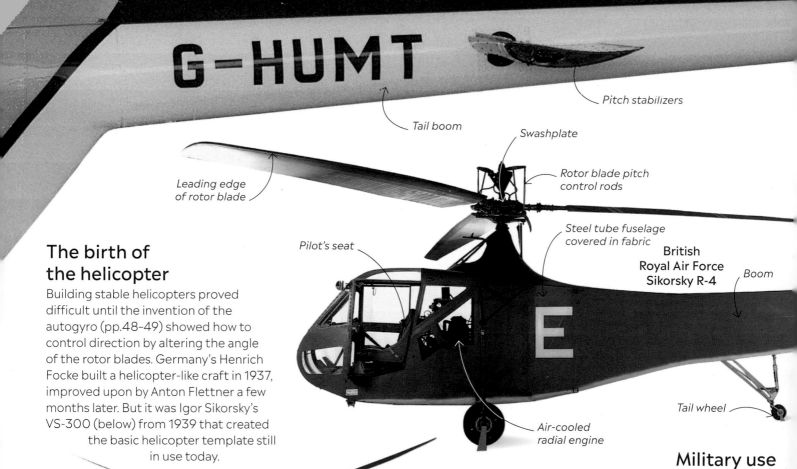

## Tail torque

Without a tail rotor, a helicopter's fuselage would spin around in the opposite direction to the torque (twisting force) exerted by the main rotor as it spins. To control this, helicopters use thrust from the tail rotor to balance out the torque. The pilot adjusts the variable-pitch blades using "rudder" or torque pedals.

*Tail rotor*

## Sikorsky R-4 1945

After creating his breakthrough VS-300 helicopter in 1939, airplane designer Igor Sikorsky went on to design the R-4 helicopter (below), of which more than 400 had been built for the USAAF by the end of World War II.

*Tail fin*

*Tail rotor pitch control wires*

KK995

*Blades made of carbon fiber provide lift in the thin Martian atmosphere.*

### 👁 EYEWITNESS

**J. (Bob) Balaram**
Balaram is an Indian American scientist and engineer who works for the NASA space agency. He designed Ingenuity, the Mars helicopter (see below), which exceeded expectations by operating not just for weeks but for years.

*Rotor blade*

## Head in a whirl

Once the practicality of the helicopter was proven in the late 1930s, people saw the possibilities for miniature, personal flying machines—including this bizarre backpack designed by Frenchman Georges Sablier. It is not known whether it ever flew.

## Flying on Mars

Delivered to Mars as payload attached to the underside of NASA's Perseverance rover, the autonomous helicopter Ingenuity became the first aircraft to make a powered, controlled flight on a planet other than Earth on April 19, 2021.

# War in the air

Soon after the first powered flights, it became clear that aircraft would play a key role in warfare. From the first aerial spies and "dogfights" in wooden biplanes of World War I, technology evolved rapidly, leading to jet fighters by the end of World War II. Military aircraft have now developed into hugely powerful machines, always at the leading edge of aviation.

*Special coatings on the canopy scatter radar waves.*

*Powerful radar identifies targets.*

*Air intakes shaped to avoid radar detection*

## World War I

Only 11 years after the first powered flight (p.14), came the first aerial combat. Rapid development saw aircraft become faster, stronger, and more heavily armed.

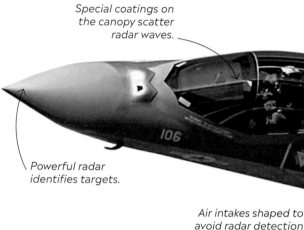

The German Fokker Dr.1 triplane was highly maneuverable.

*"Drooping" leading edge helps low-speed maneuverability.*

P51-D Mustang

## World War II

The North American P51 Mustang was one of the best fighter planes of World War II—faster, more nimble, and with a longer range than previous aircraft. More than 15,000 were built.

*Flaperons combine the functions of both flaps and ailerons.*

## Cold War

After World War II, the decades of tension between the US and the USSR were called the Cold War. Both sides built huge numbers of jet fighters, bombers, missiles, and spy planes, such as the SR-71 Blackbird, to deter each other from starting a catastrophic nuclear war.

The SR-71 Blackbird could fly at 2,193 mph (3,530 kph).

## Safety equipment

Military pilots use advanced safety and survival equipment. In an emergency, the ejection seat fires the pilot out of the aircraft so they can parachute safely to the ground. G-suits help pilots stay conscious under extreme turning forces.

*Helmet, oxygen mask, and visor*

*Parachute pack*

*Inflatable life jacket*

*Seat harness*

*Jet exhaust nozzle*

*G-suit compresses legs to stop blood pooling.*

*Ankle straps restrain legs during ejection.*

*Survival pack stored under seat*

*Movable stabilator*

## F-35

The Lockheed Martin F-35 Lightning II, has been in service since 2015. Designed to be "stealthy" to avoid detection by the enemy, the aircraft uses complex computer systems to fulfil many roles including air defense, ground strikes, and reconnaissance.

MQ-9 Reaper RPA

## Future developments

The role of remotely piloted (RPA) aircraft such as the MQ-9 Reaper has become vital in recent conflicts. Operators can fly missions with great precision from thousands of miles away.

# Hot-air balloon

Ballooning almost died out after World War I, but technological advances in the 1960s revived it. Instead of expensive helium, balloonists returned to hot air, burning liquid propane gas to inflate durable plastic-coated nylon envelopes. Today there are events around the world.

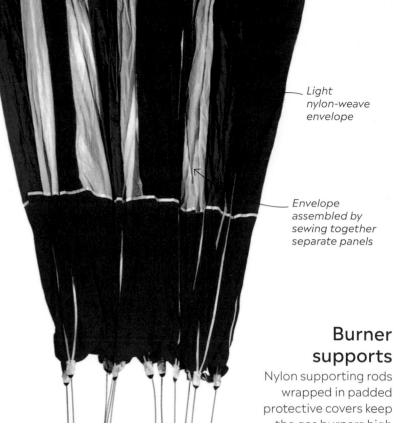

*Light nylon-weave envelope*

*Envelope assembled by sewing together separate panels*

## Burner supports
Nylon supporting rods wrapped in padded protective covers keep the gas burners high above the flyers' heads.

## The envelope
The balloon's tough nylon envelope has a crisscross weave to stop it tearing. The crown of the balloon rarely exceeds 120°C (248°F), well below nylon's melting-point, but there is a temperature sensor at the top of the envelope, just in case.

*Twin burners*

*Stainless-steel burner frame links balloon and basket.*

*Cables end in quick-release spring clips for easy assembly and dismantling.*

## Inflation
Filling the balloon is perhaps the trickiest part of a balloon flight. Here, the burner is inflating the balloon on the ground.

*Carrying handles for ground crew*

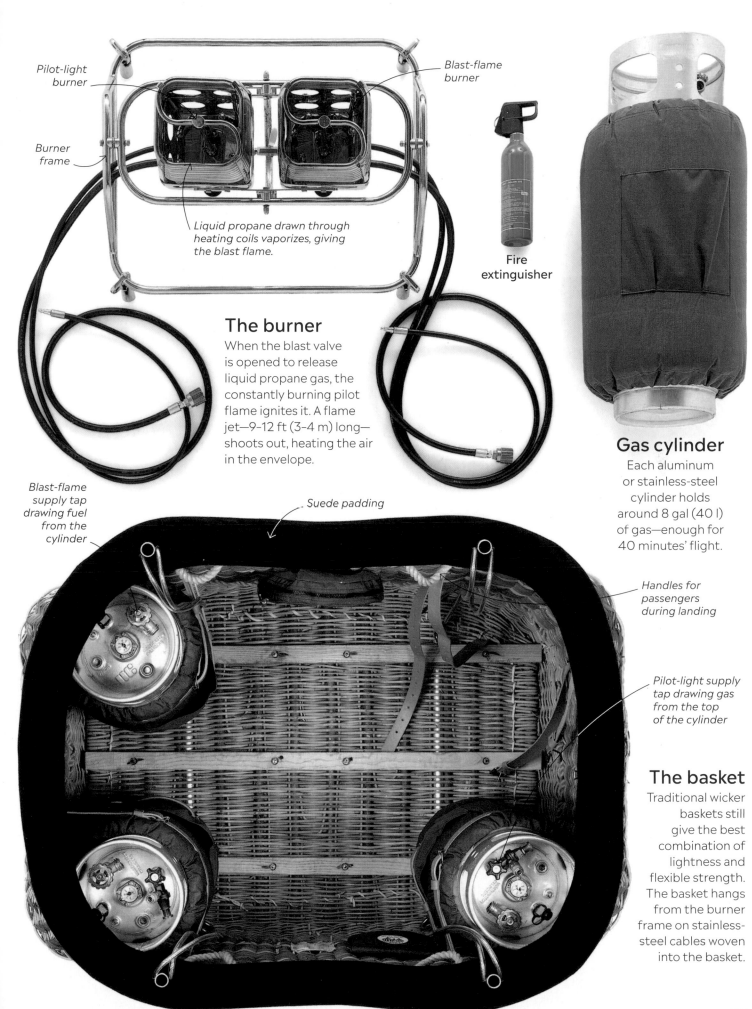

Pilot-light burner

Blast-flame burner

Burner frame

Liquid propane drawn through heating coils vaporizes, giving the blast flame.

Fire extinguisher

## The burner

When the blast valve is opened to release liquid propane gas, the constantly burning pilot flame ignites it. A flame jet—9–12 ft (3–4 m) long—shoots out, heating the air in the envelope.

Blast-flame supply tap drawing fuel from the cylinder

## Gas cylinder

Each aluminum or stainless-steel cylinder holds around 8 gal (40 l) of gas—enough for 40 minutes' flight.

Suede padding

Handles for passengers during landing

Pilot-light supply tap drawing gas from the top of the cylinder

## The basket

Traditional wicker baskets still give the best combination of lightness and flexible strength. The basket hangs from the burner frame on stainless-steel cables woven into the basket.

# Airship

The days of airships appeared to be over following several tragic accidents in the 1930s. But small, nonrigid airships called blimps, filled with nonflammable helium gas, still had their uses. In the 1980s, a new generation of airships made from carbon fiber and plastic took to the skies.

## Up in flames

The inferno that destroyed the *Hindenburg* in 1937 marked the end for giant hydrogen-filled airships.

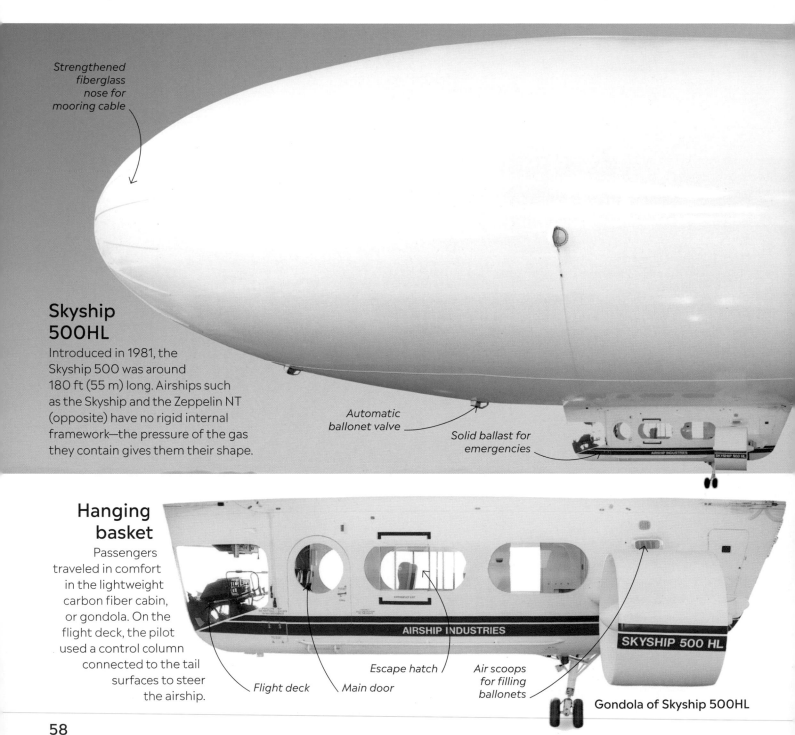

Strengthened fiberglass nose for mooring cable

## Skyship 500HL

Introduced in 1981, the Skyship 500 was around 180 ft (55 m) long. Airships such as the Skyship and the Zeppelin NT (opposite) have no rigid internal framework—the pressure of the gas they contain gives them their shape.

Automatic ballonet valve

Solid ballast for emergencies

## Hanging basket

Passengers traveled in comfort in the lightweight carbon fiber cabin, or gondola. On the flight deck, the pilot used a control column connected to the tail surfaces to steer the airship.

Flight deck

Escape hatch

Main door

Air scoops for filling ballonets

AIRSHIP INDUSTRIES

SKYSHIP 500 HL

Gondola of Skyship 500HL

## AIR BUBBLES

Helium gas in an airship expands and contracts as the vessel climbs and descends. Air-filled bags inside the envelope, called ballonets, take in or release air to compensate for this. They are also used to adjust the pitch angle of the craft by changing the centre of mass (below).

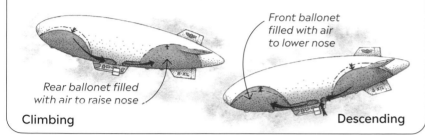

Rear ballonet filled with air to raise nose

Front ballonet filled with air to lower nose

Climbing

Descending

## Return of the Zeppelins

In 1997, Zeppelin launched its New Technology (NT) craft. Holding two crew and 12 passengers, NTs are much smaller than the Zeppelins of the 1930s, which carried more than 100 people. Nevertheless, Zeppelin NTs are the world's biggest airships today.

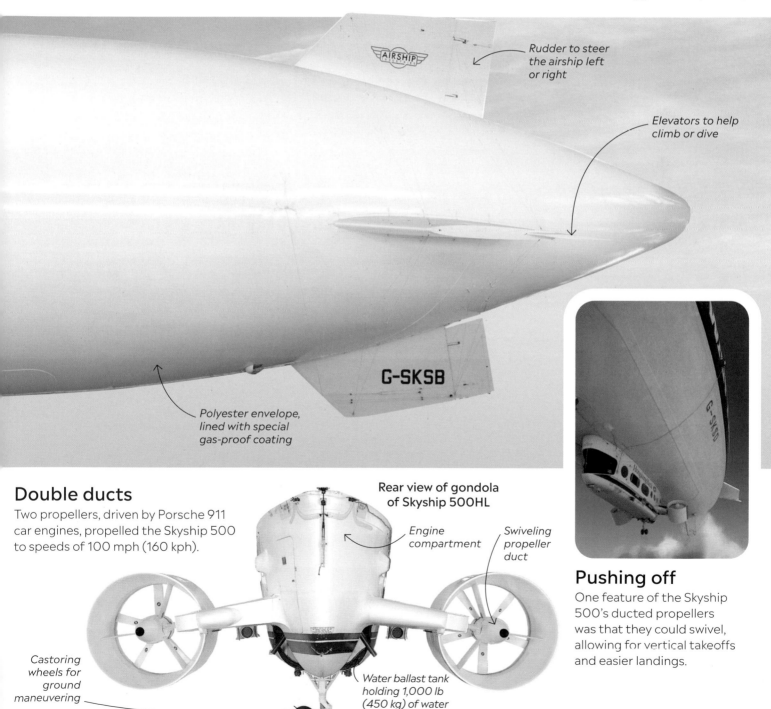

Rudder to steer the airship left or right

Elevators to help climb or dive

Polyester envelope, lined with special gas-proof coating

G-SKSB

## Double ducts

Two propellers, driven by Porsche 911 car engines, propelled the Skyship 500 to speeds of 100 mph (160 kph).

Rear view of gondola of Skyship 500HL

Engine compartment

Swiveling propeller duct

Castoring wheels for ground maneuvering

Water ballast tank holding 1,000 lb (450 kg) of water

## Pushing off

One feature of the Skyship 500's ducted propellers was that they could swivel, allowing for vertical takeoffs and easier landings.

# A modern glider

Gliders played a prominent part in the pioneering days of aviation (pp.10–11), but it was only in the 1920s that their popularity grew. This was after it was discovered they could stay aloft for hours—rather than just a few seconds, as previously—by riding on winds rising over hills and ridges, or by floating on bubbles of rising air warmed by the ground, known as thermals.

## Master glider

Birds of prey showed people how to rise up on "thermals"— bubbles of warm air.

Tug makes normal takeoff with glider in tow.

Powered tug plane tows glider.

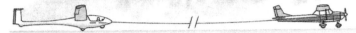

## Launching a glider

The best way to launch a glider and gain maximum height is by towing it behind a small plane (above). Using a static winch or towing behind an automobile is cheaper and quicker, but only allows the glider to reach a height of around 1,000 ft (300 m).

## Band aid

In a bungee launch, a team of people use elastic rope to catapult a glider off the edge of a hill and into the air.

## No "lift" here?

To avoid the hazards of "landing out" in areas where lift from rising air is absent, many gliders are now fitted with "sustainer" motors.

*Tow rope attaches here.*

D-KL

*Retractable, electric "self-launch" motor*

*T-tail*

33

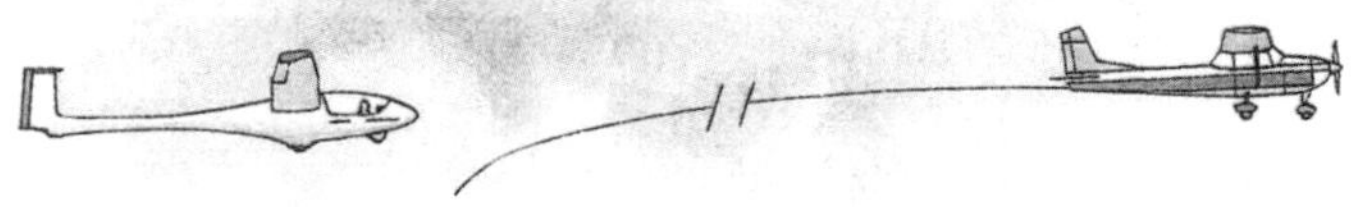

Glider releases tow rope at desired height.

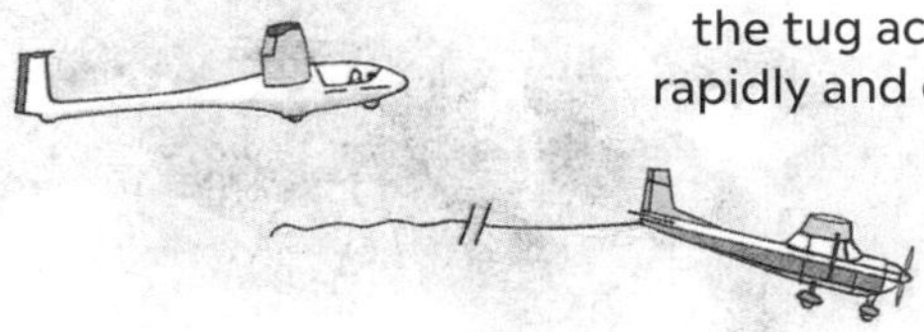

Freed from the glider, the tug accelerates rapidly and dives away.

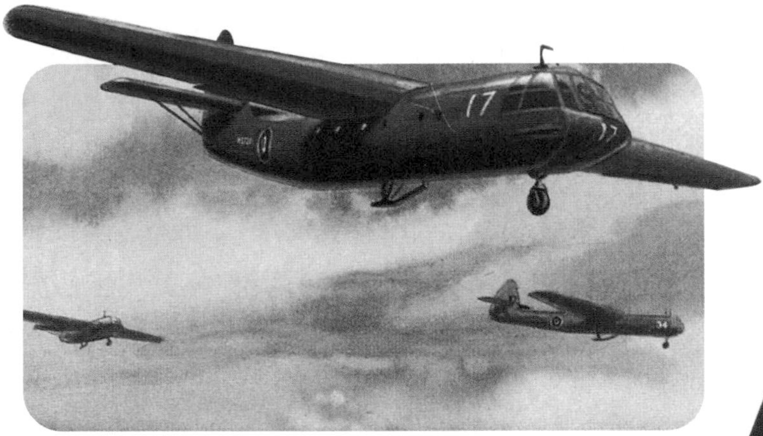

## Silent wings

Large gliders like the Airspeed Horsa (above) were used during World War II for silently landing troops and equipment behind enemy lines. But they were slow and extremely vulnerable if spotted.

### EYEWITNESS

**Richard Bomphrey**

In a return to the pioneers' study of bird flight, British biologist and engineer Richard Bomphrey observed birds of prey, such as owls and goshawks, gliding in his laboratory. Tracking the swirling air patterns created by the wings of these master gliders may offer new ideas for wing designers.

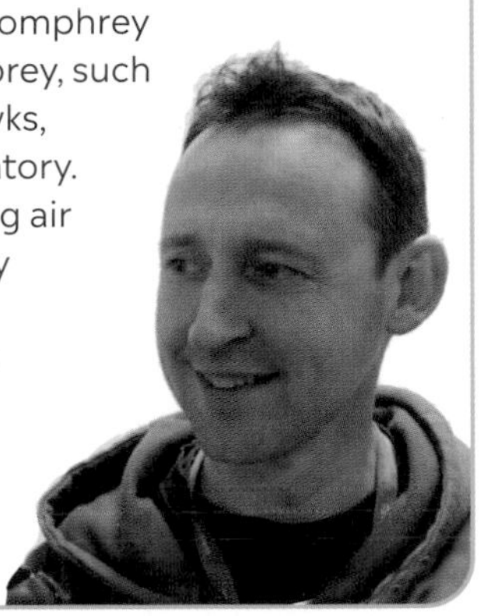

## Slender form

Glider design is all about minimizing drag. To reduce the frontal area, the pilot and passenger seats are reclined, as they are in F1 cars.

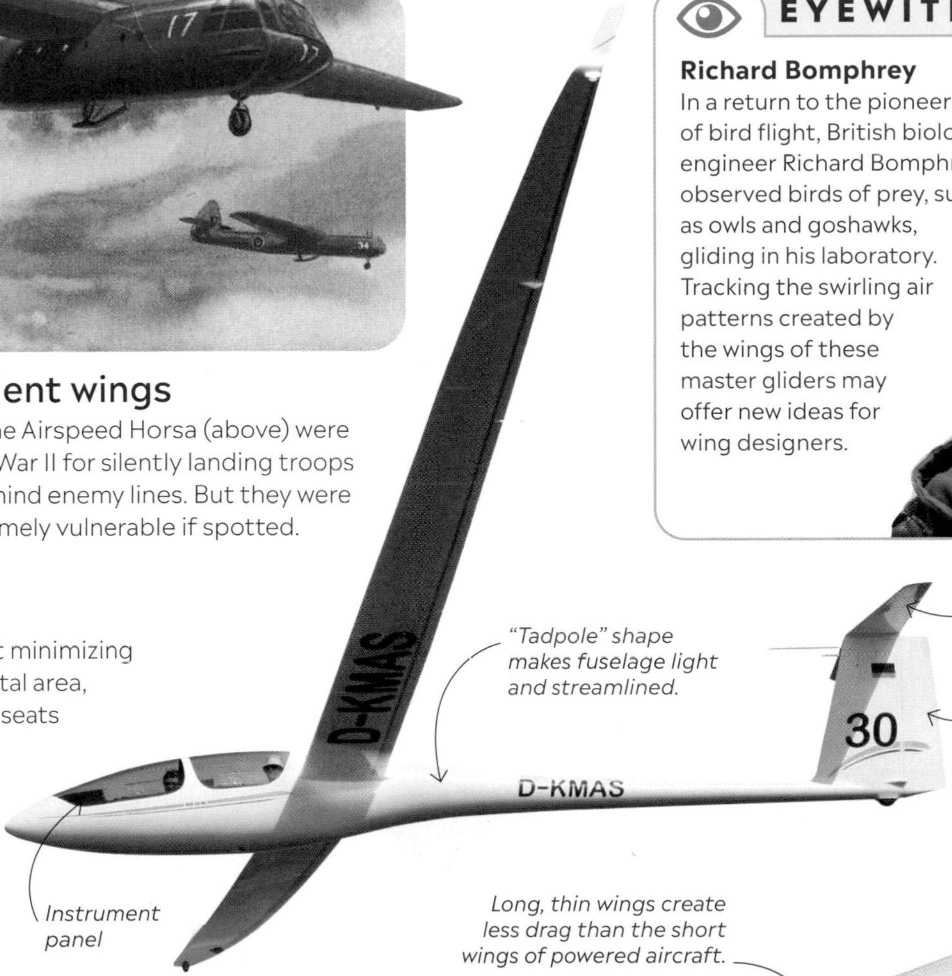

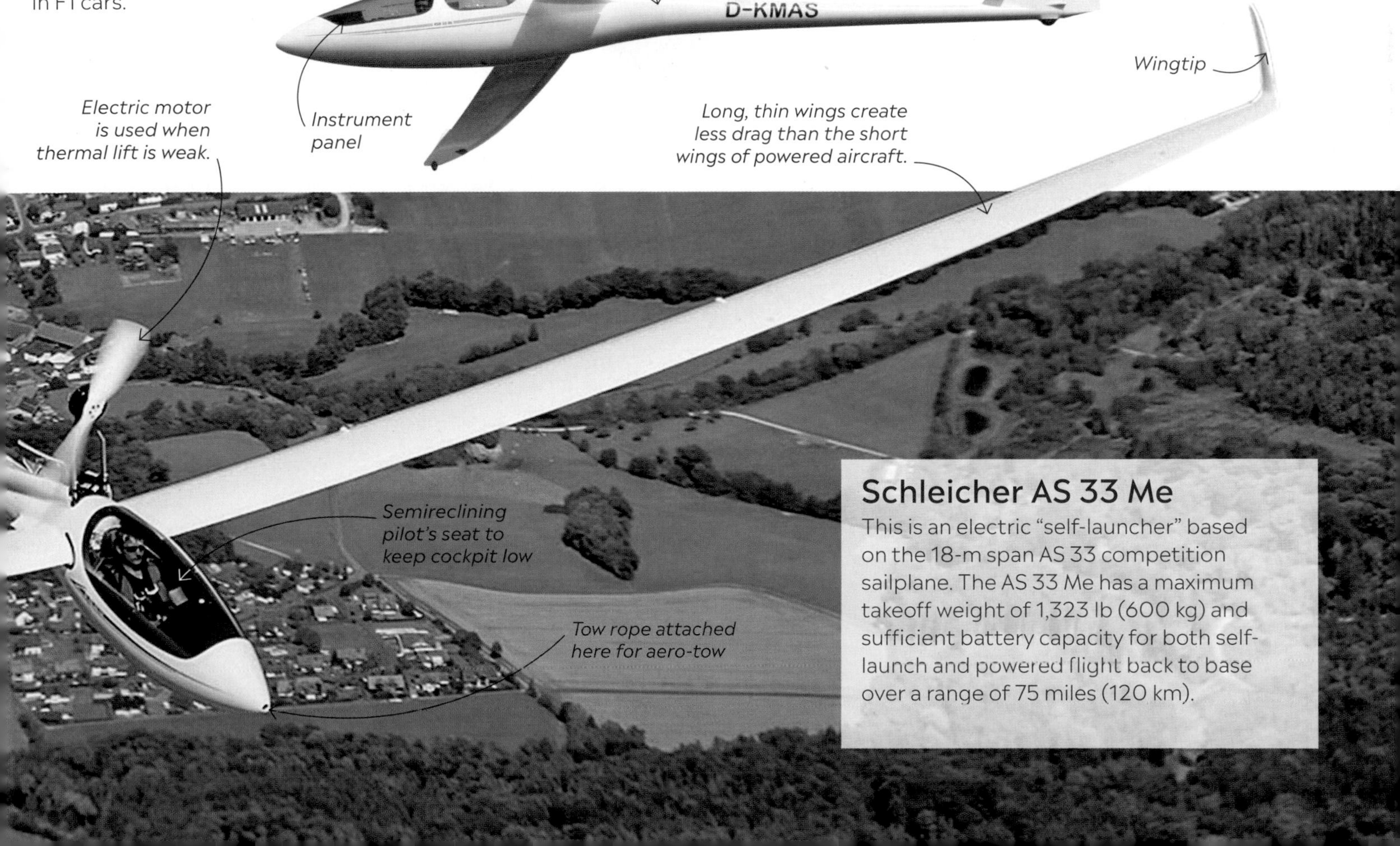

*"Tadpole" shape makes fuselage light and streamlined.*
*T-tail*
*Rudder*
D-KMAS
30
*Instrument panel*


*Wingtip*
*Long, thin wings create less drag than the short wings of powered aircraft.*
*Electric motor is used when thermal lift is weak.*
*Semireclining pilot's seat to keep cockpit low*
*Tow rope attached here for aero-tow*


## Schleicher AS 33 Me

This is an electric "self-launcher" based on the 18-m span AS 33 competition sailplane. The AS 33 Me has a maximum takeoff weight of 1,323 lb (600 kg) and sufficient battery capacity for both self-launch and powered flight back to base over a range of 75 miles (120 km).

# Plain sailing

After the invention of the airplane in 1903, the idea of flying without power went out of fashion for many years. But, in 1940, Francis Rogallo developed a steerable parachute based on a triangular wing. People began to fly these wings by hanging underneath, and hang gliding was born.

*Leading edge often reinforced with Mylar to give an aerodynamic shape*

*Aluminum or plastic wing battens stiffen the wing.*

## Spreading wings
Modern hang gliders use a variety of methods to create highly efficient wing shapes, allowing them to use thermals (rising bubbles of warm air) to make flights of more than 100 miles (160 km).

*Nose joint for leading-edge spars*

## Hanging harness
Early hang glider harnesses were adapted from climbing equipment. They have since been replaced by technically advanced body bags that are both warm and reduce drag.

## Peak performance
In mountainous areas, hang gliders can ride up ski lifts before making an exhilarating flight down the mountain to a landing area at the bottom.

*A-frame allows the pilot to control the glider.*

*Wing spars made from aluminum tubing*

**The record for the longest flight by a hang glider is 475 miles (764 km), set by Dustin Martin.**

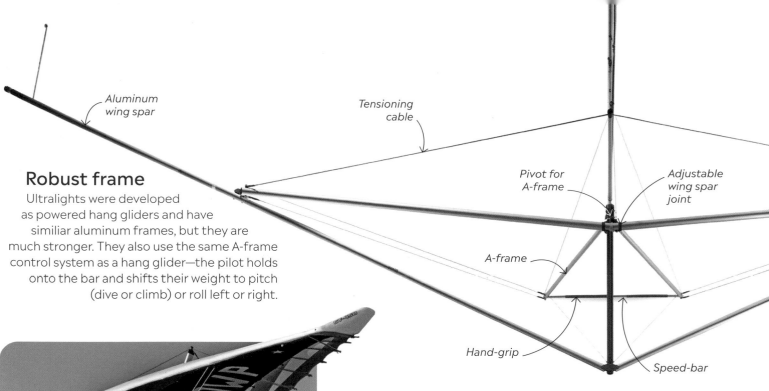

## Robust frame

Ultralights were developed as powered hang gliders and have similiar aluminum frames, but they are much stronger. They also use the same A-frame control system as a hang glider—the pilot holds onto the bar and shifts their weight to pitch (dive or climb) or roll left or right.

Aluminum wing spar

Tensioning cable

Pivot for A-frame

Adjustable wing spar joint

A-frame

Hand-grip

Speed-bar

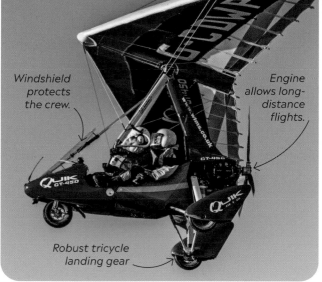

Windshield protects the crew.

Engine allows long-distance flights.

Robust tricycle landing gear

## Modern ultralight

Ultralights such as the P&M GT450 are able to carry two people 375 miles (608 km) at a cruise speed of around 80 mph (130 kph), opening up a hugely popular and relatively affordable way for people to fly.

 **EYEWITNESS**

### Zara Rutherford

In 2022, at the age of 19, Zara Rutherford became the youngest female pilot to fly solo around the world. She made the five-month journey in her Shark.Aero Shark UL, a fully enclosed ultralight not so different from a conventional light airplane (pp.26–27).

## Paragliding

The onset of steerable parachutes in the 1960s gave rise to high-tech canopies that use air to create the wing shape needed to stay aloft for long periods. The pilot is suspended in a harness and uses control lines to steer.

# Did you **know?**

## AMAZING FACTS

**Wright brothers' first powered flight**

The first passengers in a free flight were a sheep, a duck, and a rooster, which in 1783 flew in a wicker basket suspended from a balloon designed by the Montgolfier brothers.

The first aerial stowaway was a Frenchman called Fontaine, who jumped into a Montgolfier hot-air balloon as it was taking off in 1784.

The *Flyer* made four flights on December 17, 1903, with the Wright brothers taking turns. The longest flight of the day (59 seconds) was made by Wilbur, covering 853 ft (260 m).

The first woman to make a solo flight was Baroness Raymonde de Laroche, in 1909. A year later, she was the first woman to receive a pilot's license, granted by the Aéro Club of France.

The first solo flight across the Atlantic was made by Charles Lindbergh in 1927, in a Ryan monoplane called the *Spirit of St. Louis*. To stay awake throughout the 33.5-hour flight he pinched himself and opened the aircraft's side window for blasts of air.

The first helicopter flight was made by French mechanic Paul Cornu in 1907 when his machine lifted and hovered for 20 seconds.

The Blue Max (the nickname of the *Ordre pour le Mérite*, the highest German honor for service in World War I) was named after flying ace Max Immelmann.

In the early days of flying, one of the most famous awards was the Schneider Trophy. The first Schneider seaplane air race, held in Monaco in 1913, was won by Maurice Prévost, the only pilot to finish the course. His average speed was 45.7 mph (73.6 kph).

In 1929, the first all-woman air race took place in the United States, from California to Ohio. The contestants included Amelia Earhart (p.33).

The Airbus A350-900ULR can fly for 11,200 miles (18,000 km) without needing to stop to refuel.

In 1988, Kanellos Kanellopoulos made the longest muscle-powered flight in *Daedalus*—a human-powered aircraft. He pedaled 70 miles (115 km) in 4 hours.

**Charles Lindbergh**

**Schneider Trophy poster**

In 1999, the *Breitling Orbiter 3,* piloted by Bertrand Piccard and Brian Jones, became the first balloon to fly nonstop around the world. In 2002, American Steve Fossett did this solo, taking 13 days in the *Spirit of Freedom* balloon.

Steve Fossett also made the fastest solo plane flight around the world, in 67 hours and 2 minutes, in 2006. The fastest team circumnavigation was made in 2010 by Swiss aviator Riccardo Mortara and two crewmates. They did it in 57 hours and 54 minutes.

**Steve Fossett**

Stratolaunch
aircraft

# QUESTIONS AND ANSWERS

## Who was the first person in history to fly?

The first person to fly in free flight was Jean-François Pilâtre de Rozier, who, accompanied by the Marquis d'Arlandes, flew for 23 minutes and traveled 5.5 miles (9 km) in a Montgolfier balloon on November 21, 1783. However, the world's first aviator is considered to be Otto Lilienthal, who invented a practical hang glider and became the first person to make repeated controlled flights in the early 1890s. Orville Wright made the world's first powered airplane flight on December 17, 1903, at Kitty Hawk in North Carolina, in the *Flyer*. The flight lasted a mere 12 seconds, and the aircraft traveled just 120 ft (37 m).

Airbus A380

## What is the world's largest passenger plane?

The Airbus A380 made its maiden flight in 2005, and entered service in 2007 with Singapore Airlines. It has a wingspan of almost 262 ft (80 m) and floor space of about 3,450 sq ft (320 sq m)—49 percent more than the next largest airliner, the Boeing 747-400. The A380 can seat 525 people in a typical three-class configuration or up to 853 people in all-economy class configurations.

## How did the first aviators manage to find their way?

The first airplanes had no instruments, so to find out where they were, aviators simply looked out of the plane for landmarks, such as a church tower or railway line. To find their height, they had small pocket altimeters similar to those used by mountaineers.

## Why are the blades of an aircraft propeller twisted?

Propeller blades spin faster at the tips than at the center. Twisting the blade ensures that uniform thrust is produced along its entire length, even though different parts of it are spinning at different speeds.

## Why was Concorde not universally welcomed?

Despite being the fastest airliner ever, Concorde was banned from some airports because its turbojets were very noisy during takeoff and landing. It was barred from flying at supersonic speeds over land because of the "sonic boom" it made when flying faster than the speed of sound.

Hartsfield–Jackson International Airport, Atlanta, Georgia

Concorde

# Timeline

Since the earliest days of flight, aviators have often made headlines with records for speed, altitude, and endurance. But less-celebrated figures have been just as important, turning flight into a safe and reliable form of transport.

American pilot Eugene Ely

### Dreams of flight

Humans look to the skies with little idea how to fly—Daedalus and Icarus in myth, Abbas ibn Firnas in legend, and Leonardo da Vinci in drawings.

### Balloon 1783

In France, papermakers Joseph and Jacques Montgolfier build a hot-air balloon to float across Paris. Weeks later, physicist Jacques Charles' hydrogen balloon soars to 2,000 ft (610 m) high.

### Airship 1852

French engineer and inventor Henri Giffard fixes a steam engine and propeller to a streamlined hydrogen balloon, creating an airship.

### Glider 1853

Englishman Sir George Cayley builds the world's first steerable glider. His terrified coachman reluctantly pilots the craft, but quits, saying he was "hired to drive, not to fly."

### Internal combustion engine 1885

German engineers Gottlieb Daimler and Wilhelm Maybach build a new gas-driven engine. It is the first that is small and light enough to fit into aircraft.

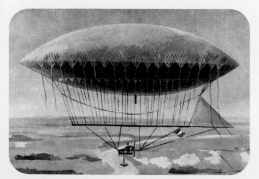

Henri Giffard's airship

### Hang glider 1891

German engineer Otto Lilienthal makes the first of many flights in pioneering hang gliders. His work inspires others (pp.10–11).

### Heavier-than-air flight 1903

Americans Orville and Wilbur Wright make the first sustained, controlled flight in a powered aircraft that is heavier than air, at Kill Devil Hills, North Carolina (pp.10–15).

The Wright brothers' *Flyer*

### Duralumin 1908

German metallurgist Alfred Wilm blends aluminum with copper and magnesium to create Duralumin. It is strong, hard, and light—an ideal material for building aircraft.

### Channel crossing 1909

French airman Louis Blériot makes the first airplane crossing of the English Channel (p.14).

### Seaplane 1910

American engineer Glenn Curtiss fixes a canoe to the underside of a plane to make a practical seaplane.

### Flying from ships 1910

American pilot Eugene Ely takes off from the deck of a battleship in a Curtiss Albany Flyer.

### Bombing flight 1911

Air warfare begins when Lt Giulio Gavotti of the Italian Army Aviation Corps drops grenades onto Turkish troops in Libya. Nobody is hurt.

### Autopilot 1914

American inventor Lawrence Sperry shows off the first automatic pilot, with a gyroscope to keep the plane level.

### Passenger service 1914

The world's first air passenger service links Tampa and St. Petersburg, in Florida. It costs $5 to fly 20 miles (32 km) across the bay in a flying boat.

### Air traffic control 1920

Croydon Airport near London, UK, builds the first "aerodrome control tower" to assist pilots.

### Radial engine 1925

The Wright J-5 Whirlwind is much easier to handle than rotary engines, and is light and powerful.

### Nonstop Atlantic crossing 1927

Charles Lindbergh flies his Ryan NYP from New York to Paris—the first solo nonstop flight across the Atlantic Ocean (p.26).

### Flying with instruments 1929

American pilot Jimmy Doolittle takes off, flies 15 miles (25 km), and lands, all with an opaque fabric hood over the cockpit. He proves pilots can fly in fog and cloud, using instruments alone.

### Flight simulator 1930

American organ builder Edwin Link creates the first flight simulator for safer pilot training. The model cockpit tilts in response to the controls.

### Transatlantic flight by a woman 1932

American aviator Amelia Earhart flies alone across the Atlantic in a Lockheed Vega in less than 15 hours.

### Monocoque construction 1933

The Boeing 247 is one of the first airliners to have a monocoque fuselage, using a metal skin for strength instead of a rigid frame.

### Radar 1934

American physicist Dr Robert M. Page invents radio direction and ranging (RADAR). The ingenious "radio vision" can track planes in midair.

### Pressurized airliner 1938

The Boeing 307 pumps air into the passenger cabin, so that the plane can fly at high altitudes where the air is thin and the ride faster and smoother.

### Jet aircraft 1939

The Heinkel He 178 is the first aircraft to fly with a jet engine. Turbojet engines (p.37) will allow aircraft to fly higher and faster than ever before.

### Helicopter 1939

Russian-American engineer Igor Sikorsky flies his VS-300 helicopter. It is the first truly practical model, with a main and tail rotor (p.52).

### Ejector seat 1941

The experimental Heinkel He 280 jet fighter is fitted with an ejector seat, which allows the pilot to escape safely from a damaged aircraft.

### Supersonic flight 1947

US test pilot Chuck Yeager fires rocket motors to blast his Bell X-1 plane past the speed of sound (p.36).

SpaceshipOne

### Fly-by-wire 1952

The British Avro Vulcan is the first fly-by-wire aircraft. Pilot controls no longer move control surfaces directly. Instead electrical signals power motors to move them.

### Jet airliner 1952

The first jet airliner, the de Havilland Comet (p.34), carries passengers for a British airline—cruising twice as fast and high as piston-engined airliners.

### Flight data recorders 1958

The US Civil Aviation Authority rules that commercial aircraft must record key data such as speed, altitude, and engine temperature to aid crash investigators.

### Supersonic airliner 1976

British and French airlines start the first supersonic passenger services with Concorde (p.34).

Charles "Chuck" Yeager

### Solar-powered aircraft 1980

The Gossamer Penguin is the first solar-powered aircraft to fly.

### Stealth aircraft 1981

Built in the super-secret US "Skunk Works" factory, the Lockheed F-117A is the first stealth fighter.

### Remote pilot 2001

A Northrop Grumman RQ-4 Global Hawk flies nonstop from the US to Australia, the longest flight by an uncrewed aerial vehicle (UAV).

### Private space travel 2004

SpaceShipOne becomes the first privately funded craft to reach space.

### Double-decker flying 2005

The Airbus A380 successfully tests the first fully double-decker airliner, with space for up to 853 passengers.

### Electric passenger plane 2020

The Pipistrel Velis Electro is the first all-electric airplane to be approved to carry passengers.

### Flight on Mars 2021

NASA flies the "Ingenuity" helicopter on Mars—the first powered flight on another planet (p.53).

F-117A stealth fighter

# Find out more

Museums are good places to view aircraft and discover their history. Some have flight simulators you can try. Airshows and ballooning events let you see planes, hot-air balloons, airships, and military aircraft in action. The internet is a great resource for finding local events or seeing pictures from those you cannot attend.

2009 Dutch Balloon Trophy, Wezuperbrug, Netherlands

## Ballooning events

Many countries have national balloon championships and local festivals for enthusiasts. The World Ballooning Championships are held every two years.

## Take a ride

At some museums and airshows, it is possible to take to the sky in an airplane. For example, visitors to the Old Rhinebeck Aerodrome in New York State can have a ride in an open-cockpit biplane (left).

SUGAR under test at NASA

Aircraft and crowds at the 2022 Royal International Air Tattoo (RIAT), RAF Fairford, Gloucestershire, UK

## What lies ahead?

Boeing's SUGAR (Subsonic Ultra Green Aircraft Research) Volt hybrid aircraft concept combines a highly efficient "truss-braced" glider-like wing with conventional turbofans for takeoff and electric propulsion for cruising.

## Airshows

Popular public aircraft events include the Paris Airshow, first held in 1908, the Royal International Air Tattoo in Gloucestershire, UK (see left), EAA AirVenture Oshkosh in Oshkosh, Wisconsin, and Airshow London in Ontario, Canada. Most feature a mixture of stunt displays, fly-bys, and aircraft to admire on the ground.

One of the Red Arrows' Hawk T1 jet trainer aircraft

## USEFUL WEBSITES

- Videos of U.S. Navy Blue Angels performances:
  **www.dvidshub.net/unit/nfds**
- News about Airbus and its planes:
  **www.airbus.com/**
- News about Boeing and its planes:
  **www.boeing.com/**
- The RAF Museum's timeline of aviation history:
  **https://www.rafmuseum.org.uk**
- Details of balloons and ballooning history:
  **www.eballoon.org/**

## Aerial displays

One of the most famous aeronautical teams is the British Royal Air Force's Red Arrows. You can see them in action and discover more at www.raf.mod.uk/display-teams/red-arrows/

## Hands-on

Flight simulator, Aviodrome Aerospace Museum, The Netherlands, 2013

Many aviation museums feature immersive flight experiences where visitors can feel the thrill of flying aboard a stunt plane or a classic fighter jet. Simulators go one step further by letting you take control of a virtual plane.

## Plane-spotting

Many airports have areas where visitors can watch planes land, refuel, and take off. Some enthusiasts like to spot particular types of planes, or look out for distinctive insignia and colors. At busy airports, up to 50 aircraft take off and land every hour.

## MUSEUMS TO VISIT

**SMITHSONIAN INSTITUTION NATIONAL AIR AND SPACE MUSEUM, WASHINGTON, DC, AND CHANTILLY, VA**
www.nasm.si.edu/
This huge museum spans two locations featuring hundreds of the world's most significant objects in aviation and space history. Free timed-entry passes are required for the Museum in DC. Attractions include the Wright 1903 *Flyer*, the Ryan *Spirit of St. Louis*, and the Bell X-1.

**NATIONAL MUSEUM OF THE UNITED STATES AIR FORCE, DAYTON, OH**
www.nationalmuseum.af.mil/
The world's largest military aviation museum. The museum features more than 350 aerospace vehicles and missiles and thousands of artifacts amid more than 19 acres of indoor exhibit space. Popular exhibits include the Early Years Gallery (featuring flight pioneers and World War I planes, engines, and weapons), the World War II Gallery (including *Bockscar* and the *Memphis Belle*), and the Presidential Gallery (featuring walk-throughs of four former presidential aircraft).

**NATIONAL NAVAL AVIATION MUSEUM, PENSACOLA, FL**
navalaviationmuseum.org/
The world's largest Naval Aviation museum. It includes more than 150 beautifully restored aircraft representing Navy, Marine Corps, and Coast Guard aviation. These historic and one-of-a-kind aircraft are displayed both inside the museum's over 350,000 square feet of exhibit space and outside on its 37-acre grounds.

**AIR ZOO, KALAMAZOO, MI**
navalaviationmuseum.org/
The Kalamazoo Air Zoo features more than 100 rare and historic air and space artifacts, amusement park-style rides, Full-Motion Flight Simulators, as well as historical exhibits and educational activities.

Model of the Wright brothers' *Flyer*

# Glossary

Airship: ABC Lightship A-60+, 1994

**AERODYNAMICS** The study of the movement of objects through air.

**AEROFOIL** Curved wing shape in which the upper surface is longer (from leading to trailing edge) than the lower surface.

**AILERONS** Paired flaps on a wing's trailing edge enabling an airplane to tilt to one side (rolling or banking).

**AIRBRAKE** Surface that can be extended from an aircraft to slow it down or steepen its descent.

**AIRSHIP** Long, thin, lighter-than-air craft usually filled with helium or hot air; often steered by swiveling propellers.

**ALTIMETER** Instrument to measure an airplane's altitude.

**ARTIFICIAL HORIZON** Instrument used to indicate an aircraft's position in relation to the horizon. Today called an attitude indicator.

**AUTOGYRO** Craft with a conventional propeller and also a rotor that is spun by the action of air flowing through its disc from below; forerunner of the helicopter.

**AUTOMATIC PILOT** Also called an autopilot, an electronic system that automatically stabilizes an aircraft and allows it to follow a certain course.

**BALLONET** Air-filled compartment inside an airship (which contains lighter-than-air helium). It lets air out or in to control the airship's height.

**BIPLANE** Aircraft with two fixed wings.

**BOGIE** Type of landing leg on an aircraft with two or more pairs of wheels.

**CAMBER** Curve on the wing section of an airplane.

**CARBURETOR** Device to mix fuel with air before it enters an engine.

**COCKPIT** Compartment in a plane's fuselage for the pilot(s) and crew.

**DIRIGIBLE** Another name for an airship.

**DOPE** Airplane varnish painted onto fabric to make it stronger and tighter.

**DRAG** Pressure of air slowing down an airplane when in flight.

**DRIFT INDICATOR** Instrument that shows an airplane's angle of drift (its sideways movement in a crosswind).

**ELEVATOR** Flap on a plane's tail that enables the plane to point up or down (called pitching).

**ELEVON** Combines the functions of ailerons and elevators into one set of control surfaces.

Eurocopter HH-65 Dolphin

**ENVELOPE** Airship casing (often nylon) containing the gas that provides lift.

**FLAP** Hinged surface that is lowered to help aircraft to fly at lower speeds.

**FLEXWING** Powered hang glider with a small engine and an open fiberglass car called a trike. Ultralights are known as microlights in the UK.

**FLYING BOAT** Airplane with a watertight hull, which allows it to operate from water.

**FUSELAGE** Body of an aircraft; from the French *fuseler*, "to shape like a spindle."

**GLASS COCKPIT** Cockpit in which traditional instruments such as dials are replaced by electronic displays.

**GLIDE RATIO** How far forward an aircraft travels for every unit of height it descends when it is gliding unpowered.

**GLIDER** Unpowered aircraft with a wide wingspan that uses currents of hot, rising air (thermals) to stay airborne.

**GONDOLA** The cabin of an airship, in which the passengers and crew travel.

**HANG GLIDER** Unpowered craft that uses thermals for lift, made of material stretched across a frame to form a wing.

**HELICOPTER** Aircraft powered, lifted, and steered by rotating blades. A helicopter can take off vertically, fly slowly, hover, and move in any direction.

**HOT-AIR BALLOON** Lighter-than-air craft. Modern hot-air balloons use propane burners to heat air in the envelope (see also ENVELOPE).

**JOYSTICK** Control column used to steer an aircraft so it can dive, climb, or roll.

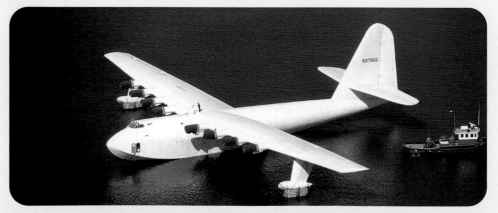

Hughes H-4 Hercules flying boat, the *Spruce Goose*, 1947

**LEADING EDGE** The front edge of (for example) a wing, rotor, or tail.

**LIFT** Upward force created by the way air flows around an aircraft wing.

**LONGERON** Part of an aircraft's structure that runs the length of the fuselage.

**MACH NUMBER** Ratio of an airplane's air speed to the velocity of sound, or speed of sound; named after the Austrian physicist Ernst Mach (1838–1916). Mach 1 is the speed of sound, or about 659 mph (1,060 kph) at 36,000 ft (11,000 m).

**MONOCOQUE** Fuselage with no internal bracing, in which nearly all the structural load is carried by the skin.

Solar Wings Pegasus Flexwing Ultralight, 1989

**MONOPLANE** Aircraft with a single wing.

**NONRIGID** Airship with no internal framework, in which shape is maintained by the pressure of gas and air ballonets inside.

**ORNITHOPTER** Aircraft propelled by flapping wings.

**PITCH** Rotating or tilting of an aircraft nose-up and nose-down by raising or lowering the elevators on the tailplane.

**PROPELLER** Rotating blades that drive an aircraft forward.

**RIGID** Airship with an internal framework.

**ROLL** Movement of an aircraft in which one wing tip rises and the other falls; roll is controlled by adjusting the ailerons.

**RUDDER** Vertical, flat surface for yawing an airplane to the right or left.

**SPAR** Structural support in a wing, running the length of the wing.

**SPEED OF SOUND** Around 761 mph (1,225 kph) at sea level, but falls the higher you go. Above an altitude of around 3,280 ft (1,000 m) the speed of sound stays the same, at about 659 mph (1,060 kph).

**STALL** When an aircraft loses lift, causing the plane to pitch downward and possibly go into a spin.

**STRUT** Vertical support or brace that strengthens the plane; for example, between the longerons in a fuselage (see also FUSELAGE, LONGERON).

**SUPERCHARGER** Device that forces extra air into an airplane's engine to increase power at high altitudes.

**SUPERSONIC** Faster than the speed of sound.

**TAILPLANE** Surface at the back of an aircraft to provide stability when pitching and to which the elevators are often attached (see also PITCH).

**TILT-ROTOR** Aircraft with rotors that enable it to take off vertically, then swivel to power the plane forward.

**TRAILING EDGE** The rear edge of (for example) a wing, rotor, or tail.

**TRIPLANE** Fixed-wing aircraft with three wings, such as the German Fokker Triplane of the early 1900s.

**TURBOFAN** Type of gas-turbine engine in which some of the power drives a fan that pushes out air with the exhaust, increasing thrust. Turbofans are used in most modern airliners because they are more economical and less noisy than turbojet engines.

Avro Triplane IV, 1910

**TURBOJET** Simple type of gas-turbine (jet) engine in which a compressor forces air into a combustion chamber, where fuel is burned, and the hot gases produced spin a turbine that drives the compressor. Turbojets are noisier than the turbofans used by most airliners. Concorde was powered by turbojets.

**TURBOPROP** Type of gas turbine engine connected to a propeller and used to power it (see also PROPELLER).

**VECTORED THRUST** Way of moving an aircraft by swiveling its propellers or the tailpipe of its jet engine so that the thrust pushes the aircraft in another direction. Some airships and fighter planes use vectored thrust.

**WIDE-BODIED** Name given to commercial airplanes with more than one aisle, allowing for three sets of seating in each row and two aisles between the sets.

**WING-WARPING** Way of controlling an airplane's ability to bank or roll by torsion (twisting) of the outer wing edges instead of using ailerons.

**YAW** Turning movement to one side or the other made by adjusting an aircraft's rudder.

Interior of a Boeing 747-8, a wide-bodied aircraft, 2011

# Index

# Acknowledgments

**The publisher would like to thank the following people for their help with making the book:**
Aeromega Helicopters, Stapleford, England: pp.50–51, 52–53; Airship Industries, London: pp.58–59, and especially Paul Davie and Sam Eller; Bristol Old Vic Theatre, Bristol, England, for studio space: pp.56–57, 63, and especially Stephen Rebbeck; Cameron Balloons, Bristol, England: pp.56–57, and especially Alan Noble; Musée des Ballons, Forbes' Chateau de Balleroy, Calvados, France: pp.8–9; RAF Museum, Hendon, London: pp.16–17, 23, 24, 29, 38–39, 48–49, 52–53, and especially Mike Tagg; SkySport Engineering, Sandy, Bedford, England: pp.18–19, 20–21; Tim Moore and all the team at SkySport; Rolls-Royce, Derby, England, pp.36–37; Solar Wings Limited, Marlborough, England: 63, and especially John Fack; The Hayward Gallery, London, and Tetra Associates: pp.6–7; The Science Museum, London: pp.10–11, 12–13, 25, 28–29, 30–31, 39, 40, 46–47, and especially Peter Fitzgerald; The Science Museum, Wroughton, England: p.33, and especially Arthur Horsman and Ross Sharp; The Shuttleworth Collection, Old Warden Aerodrome, Bedford, England: 15, 22, 38, 40–41, 42–43; and especially Peter Symes; John Bagley of the Science Museum for his help with the text; Lester Cheeseman for his desktop publishing expertise; Ian Graham for his assistance on the paperback edition; Neha Ruth Samuel for editorial assistance; Juhi Sheth for jacket design; Hazel Beynon for proofreading; and Elizabeth Wise for the index.

**Illustration** Mick Loates, Peter Bull
**Wallchart** Peter Radcliffe, Steve Setford

The publisher would like to thank the following for their kind permission to reproduce their images: (a=above, b=below/bottom, c=center, f=far, l=left, r=right, t=top)

**123RF.com:** Czgur 20bc; **Airbus:** Master Films – Hervé Goussé 44–45c; **Airship Industries:** 59br; **AirTeamImages.com:** Matthieu Douhaire 37cr, Yochai 36–37tc; **Alamy Stock Photo:** Abaca Press 35cla, Agefotostock / Michele Wassell 67tr, Aviation History Collection 39tr, 67cb, Ceri Breeze 35tl, Ryan Carter 63crb, Chronicle 39bl, 52cra, Everett Collection Historical 64bl, Malcolm Fife 34crb, 65br, GRANGER - Historical Picture Archive 8cl, 66tr, Malcolm Haines 20–21t, Imaginechina Limited 35crb, Interfoto / History 8tl, Frans Lemmens 69cl, Lordprice Collection 18cl, MediaWorldImages 3cl, 63cl, NASA Photo 55tr, PA Images 37br, PA Images / Ben Birchall 68bl, Pictorial Press Ltd 66bl, Riccardo Mancioli Archive & Historical 34cla, Sipa US 3c, Stocktrek Images, Inc. / HIGH-G Productions 67b, Sddeutsche Zeitung Photo / Scherl 48br, The Granger Collection 8cl (JOSEPH-MICHEL), Thierry GRUN – Aero 59tr, Peter Titmuss 65crb, David Wall 43tr, Andrew Walters 34–35b, World History Archive 58tl, www.jetphotos.co.uk 49bl, ZUMA Press, Inc. 65tl; **Alexander Schleicher GmbH & Co:** 60cb, 60–61b, 61c; **Austin J. Brown:** 27tl, 36cr, 57cl; **Bennie Bos**/www.hotair.nl 68tl; **(c) BRP-Rotax GmbH & Co KG:** 29br; **Corbis:** Stefano Rellandini/Reuters 52br, Galen Rowell 70tr, Karl Weatherly 70tl; **Courtesy of lilianbland.ie:** 14br; **Damien Burke**/HandmadeByMachine.com/photographersdirect. com: 69clb; **Dorling Kindersley:** Shuttleworth Collection, Bedfordshire / Martin Cameron 71tr; **Dreamstime.com:** Evren Kalinbacak 54b; **Fred**

**Sgrosso:** 68cra; **Getty Images:** Archive Photos / Bob Riha Jr 70bl, Bettmann 33bc, 53cra, Corbis Historical / Hulton Deutsch 32–33t, Jonathan Daniel 65clb, Getty Images Sport / Carl De Souza 64br, Rolls-Royce Archive 25bc, Hulton Archive / Crouch 48tl, Image Source / Nick Dolding 35tr, Photonews 63bc, Popperfoto / Paul Popper 11tr, Bill Ross 62bl, Science & Society Picture Library 12crb, 42br, SSPL / Daily Herald Archive 15bl, Stringer / Isaac Brekken 55br, Universal Images Group Editorial / UGC 54–55c; **Getty Images / iStock:** DigitalVision Vectors / Clu 9tl, Kool99 2cra, 47br, Lechatnoir 58–59c; **Hartzell Propeller LLC, Piqua Ohio, USA:** 31br; **Image courtesy of Cirrus Aircraft:** 26cla, 27tr, 26–27b; **Jerry Young:** 57bl; **Julian Herzog:** 14–15t; **Mary Evans Picture Library:** 6tc, 8bl, 11br, 15lc, 21cr, 21br, 26tl, 32cr, 33br, 39br, 52tl, 64tr; **Michael Holford:** 10tc; **NASA:** 68crb; **NASA/JPL-Caltech:** 53tr, 53b; **Photograph No. #66645; "Passport Application for Lucean Arthur Headen," September 1917; Department of State Passport Applications (Record Group 59), National Archives and Records Administration—College Park, MD.:** 47cb; **Richard Bomphrey:** 59cra; **Science Museum/ Science & Society Picture Library:** 10bl, 12bc, 13bl; **Shutterstock.com:** BestPhotoPlus 71br, Edward R 46br, Kelvin 55cr, Mny-Jhee 62c, Str / EPA 56bc; **TopFoto:** 64tl; **Yusuf Tolga Ünker:** 6bl

All other images © Dorling Kindersley

# DK WHAT WILL YOU EYEWITNESS NEXT?

 THE AMAZON

 AMERICAN REVOLUTION

 ANCIENT EGYPT

 ANCIENT GREECE

 ANCIENT ROME

 BIRD

 CAT

 THE CIVIL WAR

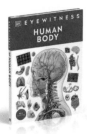 CLIMATE CHANGE

 CRYSTAL & GEM

 DINOSAUR

 THE ELEMENTS

 FISH

 FLIGHT

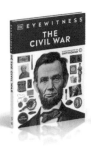 FOSSIL

 HUMAN BODY

 HURRICANE & TORNADO

 INSECT

 NATIONAL PARKS

 NATURAL DISASTERS

 OCEAN

 PLANETS

 REPTILE

 ROCKS & MINERALS

 SHARK

 SOCCER

 TITANIC

 TRAIN

 UNIVERSE

 VIKING

 VOLCANO & EARTHQUAKE

 WEATHER

 WONDERS OF THE WORLD

 WORLD WAR I

 WORLD WAR II

## Also available:

Eyewitness Amphibian
Eyewitness Ancient China
Eyewitness Ancient Civilizations
Eyewitness Animal
Eyewitness Arms and Armor
Eyewitness Astronomy
Eyewitness Aztec, Inca & Maya
Eyewitness Baseball

Eyewitness Bible Lands
Eyewitness Car
Eyewitness Dog
Eyewitness Eagle and Birds of Prey
Eyewitness Electricity
Eyewitness Endangered Animals
Eyewitness Energy
Eyewitness Forensic Science

Eyewitness Great Scientists
Eyewitness Horse
Eyewitness Judaism
Eyewitness Knight
Eyewitness Medieval Life
Eyewitness Mesopotamia
Eyewitness Mythology
Eyewitness Plant

Eyewitness Prehistoric Life
Eyewitness Presidents
Eyewitness Religion
Eyewitness Robot
Eyewitness Shakespeare
Eyewitness Soldier
Eyewitness Space Exploration
Eyewitness Tree
Eyewitness Vietnam War